745
Bol

8460

W9-CNA-436

ST. COLETTE SCHOOL
ROLLING MEADOWS, ILLINOIS

GET CRAFTY

# CARDS AND WRAPPINGS

Vivienne Bolton

DP
DEMPSEY PARR

**Editor**
Barbara Segall

**Art Direction**
Full Steam Ahead

**Design Team**
Design Study

**Photography**
Patrick Spillane

**Photographic Co-ordinator**
Liz Spillane

**Styling**
Bianca Boulton

**Project Management**
Kate Miles

The publishers would like to thank Inscribe Ltd., Bordon, Hants. for
providing the art materials used in these projects and
Sophie Boulton for her assistance.

First published in 1998 by
Dempsey Parr
Queen Street House, 4-5 Queen Street, Bath
BA1 1HE

24681097531

Copyright © Dempsey Parr 1998

Produced by Miles Kelly Publishing Ltd
Unit 11, Bardfield Centre, Great Bardfield, Essex CM7 4SL

All rights reserved. No part of this publication may be reproduced, stored in a retrieval system, or
transmitted by any means, electronic, mechanical, photocopying, recording or otherwise, without the
prior permission of the copyright holder.

**British Library Cataloguing-in-Publication Data**
A catalogue record for this book is available from the British Library.

ISBN 1-84084-397-7

Printed in Italy

# CARDS AND WRAPPINGS

## Contents

# Sticker Fun

Decorating writing paper is a great way to make good use of a sticker collection. Stickers come in such a wide range of colors and styles, you could customize writing paper to suit almost every hobby or lifestyle. Choose brightly colored writing paper to decorate and find matching envelopes. Use a large sheet of paper to make a folder for holding your matching writing paper and envelopes. You will always be able to find them when you need to send a letter.

### You will need:

Colored paper

A selection of stickers

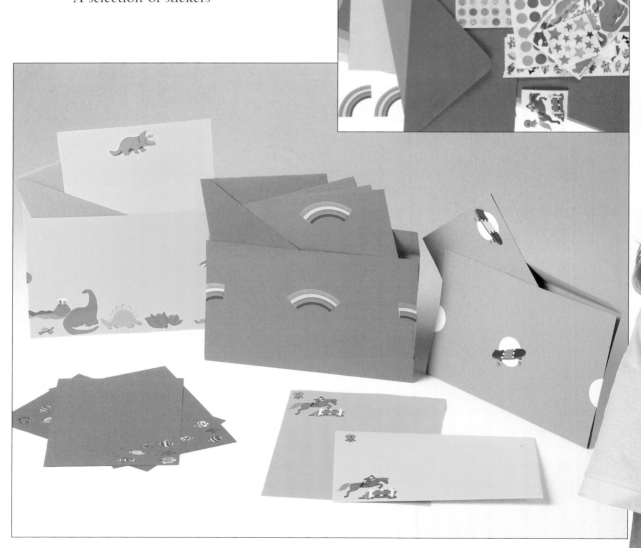

1 Choose brightly colored writing paper to make good use of the stickers. These rainbow stickers look stylish centred at the top of the page.

2 Decorate the envelopes with a sticker on the bottom left-hand corner. You could coordinate your paper and envelopes using two colors.

3 To make a folder for your decorated paper, fold up a large sheet of thin cardboard, three quarters its length, leaving a piece to fold down into a flap.

4 Hold the sides together with colorful stickers and decorate the front of the folder with matching stickers.

PAPER
# Gift Boxes

Surprise your friends with one of these stylish handmade boxes. Make small boxes from paper or slightly larger boxes from thin card. A double layer of wrapping paper would make an attractive box. Use paper that suits the gift and make a box from flowery paper to hold packets of seeds or use red paper for a Valentine box. Plain paper can be decorated with stickers or colored tape. Try decorating paper first with crayons or pencils. A set of boxes could be used to hold cake and party favors and you could personalize the boxes with your guests' names. Once you have mastered the method you will find the boxes quick and easy to make.

## You will need:
Paper

Ruler

Scissors

Glue

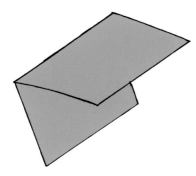

1 Fold a rectangular piece of paper in half.

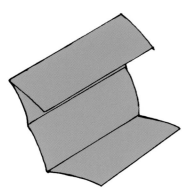

2 Fold each half in on itself, so that both ends meet in the middle.

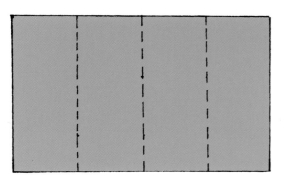

3 With the paper opened out, you will see crease marks like this.

4 Now fold the paper into thirds in the opposite direction to your first folds.

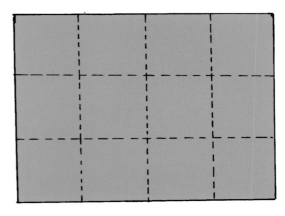

5 Now the creases should look like this.

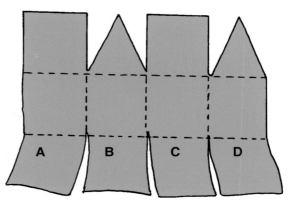

A  B  C  D

6 Cut along the crease lines and cut out the triangles as shown in the picture above.

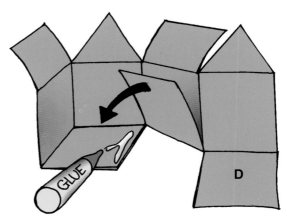

GLUE

D

7 Fold in and glue flap B onto flap A, flap C onto flap B and flap D onto flap C. Finally stick the open edge with tape on the inside and make a hole at the top of both triangles for a ribbon.

# Pop-up Cards

This pop-up card is simple to make and will brighten up someone's day. When placed on a windowsill or mantlepiece it will look as if a bunch of flowers is bursting out of the card. The cards are made and decorated with thin cardboard. If you don't have any colored thin cardboard available, cut up a cereal box and paint it in bright colors yourself.

## You will need:

Colored thin cardboard

Scissors

Glue

Colored paper

Felt tips pens

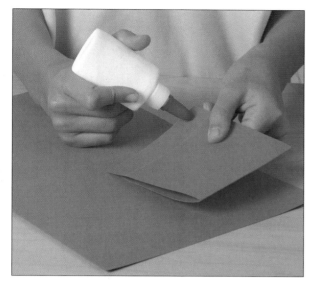

1 Begin by folding a sheet of thin cardboard in half and then open it out. Cut out a small square of cardboard and fold it in half. Fold a lip on the two edges, and glue these into the card to make the vase. Open and close the card to check that the vase flattens.

2 Using green thin cardboard, cut the stalks and leaves, use glue to attach these to the inside of the vase. Cut out some tulip-shaped flowers and glue them onto the stalks, making sure that they are hidden when the card is closed.

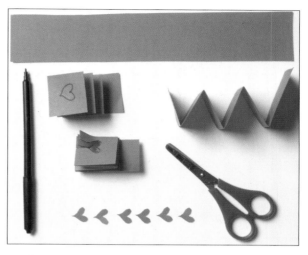

3 Cut small heart shapes to decorate the vase from red paper, folded over.

4 Now decorate the front of the card with a large red heart and a smaller blue heart, to match the rest of the design. Now you are ready to write your message on the card, using felt tip pens.

*When trying out something for the first time, start by making a rough example out of scrap paper and cardboard.*

# Bows & Ribbons

Bows and ribbons provide the final touch to a beautifully wrapped gift. You can decorate plain ribbon with felt tip pens, creating your own designs. The ribbons shown here are decorated with tiny motor vehicles and balloons, but any design would be fun. Hallowe'en pumpkins or Christmas trees are bright and easy to draw. Bows are quick to make using the method shown. Choose thin ribbon to make small bows and wider ribbon for larger bows. Coordinate the patterns and colors of your homemade bows with wrapping paper for a stylish look.

## You will need:

Ribbon

Felt-tip pens

Ruler

Scissors

Needle and thread

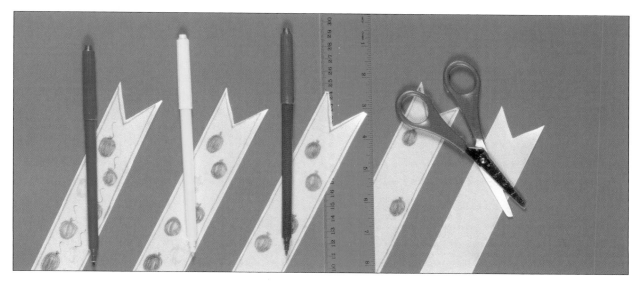

1 Use felt tip pens to decorate plain ribbon. Cut a little ribbon off to practice on. Press the pen down gently to prevent the color bleeding across the weave of the ribbon.

Complete the use of one color before moving on to the next. Remember to repeat your pattern to give the ribbon a store-bought look.

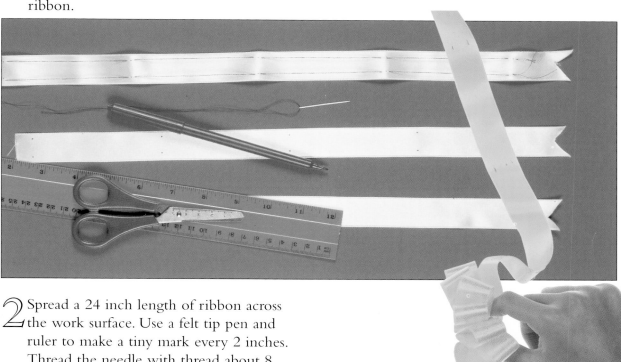

2 Spread a 24 inch length of ribbon across the work surface. Use a felt tip pen and ruler to make a tiny mark every 2 inches. Thread the needle with thread about 8 inches longer than the ribbon and make a good knot at the end. Sew a small stitch at each mark on the ribbon. Now pull gently at the thread and the ribbon should bunch up, making a fancy bow.

# Printed Cards

Spend a rainy afternoon making potato cuts to print with and you will be able to set up a production line and make a collection of cards or writing paper. The fish card is made with layers of different colored paper, each slightly smaller than the other. Cookie cutters come in lots of shapes and provide a quick way to make home made stamps. Use a small rabbit shape to decorate writing paper and envelopes. The bunch of carrots is made by first drawing the shape onto the potato half, then cutting it out with a knife. A set of cards tied with matching ribbon would make a good gift.

## You will need:

A potato

Cookie cutters

Knife

Paint and saucer

Sponge

Paper

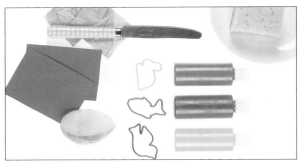

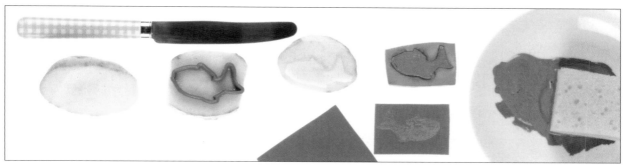

1 Begin by cutting a potato in half. Take the fish-shaped cookie cutter and press it firmly into the flesh of one half of the potato. Use the knife to cut around the shape. Lift off the cutter and remove the excess potato flesh. Put a little paint onto a saucer and use the sponge to evenly distribute the paint on the stamp. Now press the stamp gently onto blue paper. Print a few fish and leave them to dry.

2 Take a white sheet of paper and fold it in half to make the card. Now take a square of blue paper slightly smaller than the card and glue it on the front. Next glue on a small piece of gold paper. Cut out the fish print and glue it on top.

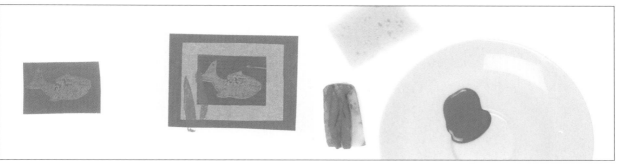

3 To finish off the picture you will need to make a simple stamp from the other half of the potato. Use the knife to cut a weed shape. Spread green paint on the stamp and print leaves of seaweed onto the card. Leave to dry.

*Protect your work surface with newspaper or a plastic cloth before you begin.*

*It is a good idea to practice stamping your design on some scrap paper to get an idea of how much paint you need to apply to the stamp.*

CARDBOARD AND PAPER
# Concertina Cards

Make one of these cards and watch the concertina movement when you open and close the card. The clown gives a good impression of playing his concertina, and the ballerina's tutu stands proudly out. The poodle's ruff looks almost real! The cards are quite simple to make, so think up some ideas of your own. You could use the concertina shape to make a bumble bee's body, or maybe a wriggly worm holding an umbrella! Use a little imagination and some brightly colored paper to create a novel concertina card for a friend's birthday.

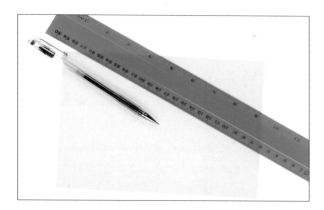

1 Fold a sheet of paper in half to form the card. Use the ruler to measure where to fix the concertina ends. Mark the two points, which should be evenly spaced on either side of the central fold.

2 Draw the clown with the arms ending at the dots. Make the picture quite simple.

3 Color in your picture with bright shades, making it as attractive as possible.

4 You will need to cut a long narrow strip of yellow paper to make the concertina. Fold it to form a fan. When folding paper always use your thumbnail to press the fold firmly down.

5 Use glue to attach each end of the concertina to the end of the clown's arms.

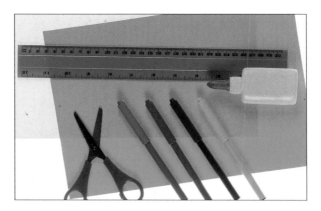

You will need:

Paper

Ruler

Felt-tip pens

Scissors

Glue

# Gift Bags

Pack your Christmas gifts in these brightly colored gift bags. You can make them almost any size. Use one layer of paper for smaller bags and a double layer to make larger bags. You could decorate the paper before you begin. Make a stencil to decorate the paper if you are making a lot of bags all to match for party favors. The bag handles can be made from string or pretty ribbon. Have a look around for paper decorated on both sides, or use gold or silver paper.

### You will need:
A selection of paper

Glue

Hole punch

Ribbon

1 Begin by folding the paper in by about one quarter of its length. Run your thumbnail along the fold to mark it well.

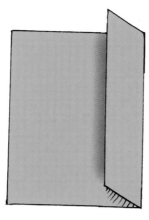
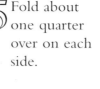

2 Turn the folded sheet of paper over and apply glue to one end.

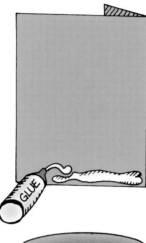

3 Glue the edges together to form a cylinder shape. Allow the glue to dry.

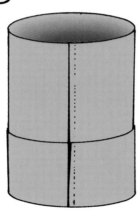

4 Flatten the cylinder shape. Run your thumbnail along the edges to make a good fold.

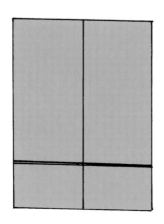

5 Fold about one quarter over on each side.

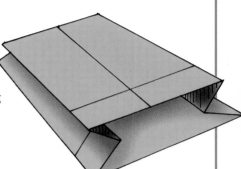

6 Open the two folds and press them inward. You should now have a bag shape.

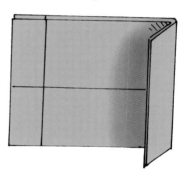

7 Make a fold upward to form the base of the bag. Glue it down.

8 Use a hole punch to make holes to thread a ribbon through and make a handle.

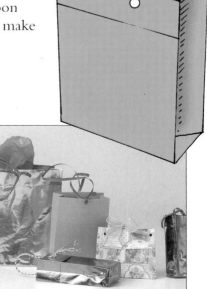

## CARDBOARD AND PAPER
# Cut-out Cards

Make a row of paper flowerpots and turn them into a birthday card, or a row of balloons to send as a party invitation. The Christmas tree cards can be decorated as brightly as you wish and the colorful fish swimming around in their bowls will brighten up the mantlepiece. Cut-out cards are quick and easy to make and decorate. When choosing the shape remember that the card will need to be cut out so draw a compact picture. A Christmas tree cut from plain white paper and decorated using a gold pen would be very stylish.

You will need:

Paper and thin cardboard

Felt-tip pens

Crayons

Scissors

Glue

Sequins to decorate

*When decorating your cards try outlining colored-in pictures with a darker shade. This will accentuate the shapes and give the cards a professional finish.*

1 This card is easy to make and fun to color, you will need a rectangle of plain white paper. Fold the sheet of paper in three to make the card shape.

2 On the front of the card draw a pot of flowers. Make sure the flower pots are joined at the lip, or the card will fall apart when you cut it out.

3 Cut away the excess paper.

4 Color in your card using bright shades.

5 To make this cheery Christmas card use a sheet of green paper folded in three. Draw on the Christmas tree shape and cut it out. Take care to leave the branches joined together at the base of the tree. Glue on small flowerpots cut from paper for the trees to stand in and decorate the Christmas trees with sequins and shiny stars, glued on.

# Notepaper

Fancy writing paper makes letterwriting more fun. You can decorate paper to suit the season: make bright sunny pictures for summer vacation letters and snowy scenes for winter times. You may like to experiment with other ideas. Maybe a seaside scene or some rolling hills covered in tiny black sheep and cows would suit a vacation mood. Choose bright coordinated colors and matching envelopes. Use the steely glints of shiny gold or silver pens to create a night scene or even to decorate a set of paper with a firework display.

## You will need:

Paper

Felt-tip pens

Scissors

Glue

1 This summery style is made from green, blue, and white sheets of paper. Decorate the sky-blue sheet of paper first. Cut out small fluffy white clouds and glue them onto the sky.

3 This snowscene is decorated with a cheerful-looking snowman. Draw the snowman onto a white sheet of paper. Remember to draw the horizon onto the page.

2 Decide how low the skyline will be and draw a wavy line across the green paper. Cut away the excess paper to leave grassy green hills. Lay one piece of paper on top of the other to create the scene.

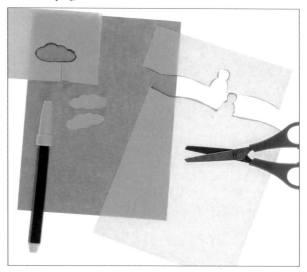

4 Use scissors to cut out the snowman and lay the sheet of white paper onto the blue sky. Decorate the snowman using a black felt-tip pen, giving him a cheerful smile.

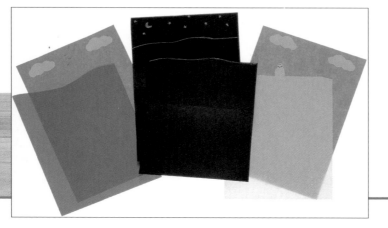

# PAPER
# Envelopes

You might have difficulty finding envelopes that are the correct size, especially if they are to match the paper and cards you have designed. Don't worry—there is no problem. Use these simple instructions and make envelopes to fit almost every size and shape of card. You could make the envelope from matching paper, patterned wrapping paper (you will need to attach a plain label for the address) or recycled paper. Decorate your home made envelopes using felt-tip pens, stickers, paint, or crayons. Remember to make the card first and use it to work around.

## You will need:
A completed card

Paper

Scissors

Glue

Felt-tip pens

*Any coloring materials should be waterproof as the envelope may get wet in the mail.*

1 Place the card in the center of the paper. Fold the paper up, over the card.

2 Fold the envelope flap down, over the card.

3 Fold in the sides. Make sure the card fits the folded shape comfortably.

4 Cut away the excess paper from the front of the envelope.

5 Cut a flap shape.

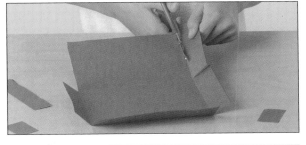

6 Use glue to hold the envelope in shape.

# Silhouettes

Making silhouettes was once a popular pastime. People would cut silhouettes in all sorts of shapes, profile outlines being very popular. Fine cutting skills are needed to make silhouettes. Practice on scraps of paper to learn the technique before you set to work on these shapes. Cut your silhouette from black paper and lay it on a light background. Try your hand at a larger silhouette, maybe a profile of yourself or a friend, to frame and hang on your bedroom wall. Silhouettes of candles and Christmas trees are very seasonal, while the pumpkin and cat cut-outs would make good Halloween party invitations.

## You will need:

Paper

Wax or pencil crayon

Scissors

Glue

1 Fold a sheet of black paper in half. Draw half a butterfly on to one side of the folded shape. Cut it out. It is possible to cut out the butterfly shape freehand.

Make a card from a folded sheet of paper and glue a piece of red paper onto the cover of the card. Glue the butterfly silhouette onto the piece of red paper.

2 This Halloween card is made with a bright yellow silhouette. Use a card made from yellow paper and glue on a black background, leaving a yellow border around the edge of the card. Fold a small piece of yellow paper in half and draw on half of the pumpkin face. Cut it out and glue it onto the black background.

# Stained Glass

**C**reate your own stained glass pictures with colored plastic wrapping. Placed where the light shines through them these cards are most effective. Colored wrapping film is available from craft shops; however, you might want to save candy wrappers and keep an eye out for colored clear plastic to recycle. The holly leaves make a good Christmas card. You can have fun decorating the card with colored glitter glue.

## You will need:

Black paper

Felt-tip pen

Scissors

Colored clear wrapping

Glue and glitter glue

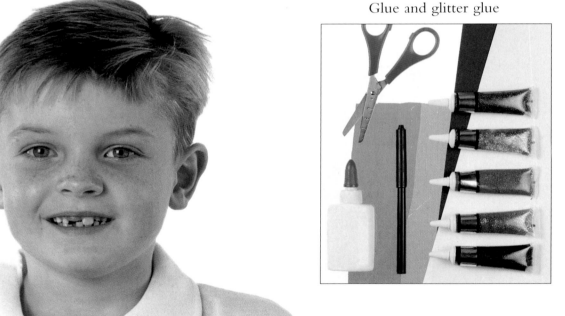

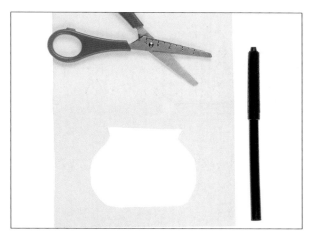

1 To make this clear blue fish bowl card begin by folding a sheet of white paper in half. Draw on a simple fish bowl shape and cut it out.

2 Cut a rectangle of blue colored wrapping slightly larger than the fish bowl. Glue the rectangle onto the inside of the card, covering the fish bowl shape.
Fold the card closed. You will decorate the cover of the card.

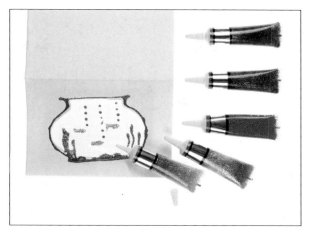

3 Use glitter glue to fill the bowl with fish, colored seaweed, and pebbles. Don't forget to paint on air bubbles. Decorate the edge of the bowl as well.

4 You will need a sheet of black paper folded in half to make the holly card. Begin by cutting out the holly leaves and berries. Cut green colored wrapping slightly larger than the cut-out leaves and glue it to the inside of the card. Use red wrapping for the berries. Fold the card to close it and decorate the stained glass-effect card with colored glitter glue.

*If you do not have glitter glue, make your own. Use ordinary glue and mix in an equal amount of fine glitter. Use a fine paintbrush to apply the glitter glue to your model or card.*

TISSUE PAPER

# Stenciled Wrapping Paper

Stenciling is a quick and effective way to decorate wrapping paper and gift tags. Use gold or silver paint to turn plain tissue paper into expensive looking wrapping paper. The stencils are easily cut from small sheets of paper folded in half. You could make matching gift wrap and tags to suit any event or gift. Once you have mastered the art of stenciling you may want to try using two colors. It is also useful to remember that other coloring materials and methods are good for stenciling. You don't have to use paint—try wax crayons, for example.

## You will need:

Paper

Pencil

Scissors

Tissue paper

Paint

Saucer

Sponge

Hole punch

Thread

*Always protect your work surface with newspaper or a vinyl cloth.*

*Remember to wipe up any spills as they happen. A good craftsperson leaves a tidy work surface.*

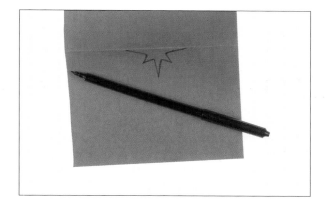

1 To make a stencil you will need a small sheet of paper. Fold it in half and draw on half of the picture, in this case half of the star, as shown in the picture above.

2 Use the scissors to cut the star out, taking care not to leave any jagged edges and not to cut into the paper. If you do, the stencil paint may come through.

3 Spread a sheet of tissue paper across your work surface. Pour a little paint onto the saucer, spread it on the sponge, damping the sponge down. Place the stencil on some rough paper and practice until you are confident.

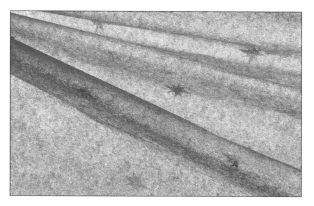

4 Stencil on the stars taking care not to smudge the paint when you lift the stencil off the paper. Hang your stenciled paper up to dry. It is a good idea to make quite a few sheets at a time, as well as matching gift tags.

5 Use paper to make these matching gift tags. Cut them out with scissors. Stencil on the star and leave to dry.

6 Use a hole punch to make a hole for the thread to tie the tag onto the gift.

## TISSUE PAPER

# Tissue Paper Cards

Tissue paper comes in such a wide range of colors, it is easy to tear and sticks with the minimum of glue. When decorating cards there is no end to the number of ways you can use tissue paper. These cards are made from torn strips of tissue and layered to create blended colors and a simple design. The colors are bright and breezy and very stylish. Have a go at layering colors yourself. Create a natural looking landscape with torn or cut greens, blues and browns.

## You will need:

Colored paper

Tissue paper

Scissors

Glue

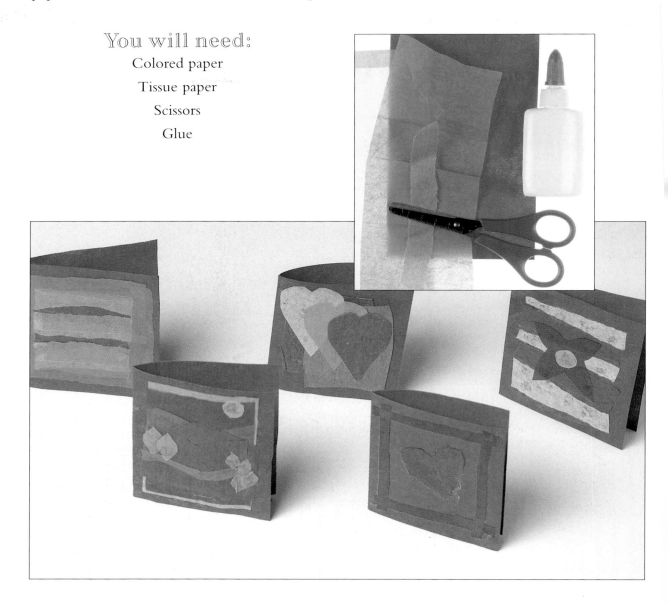

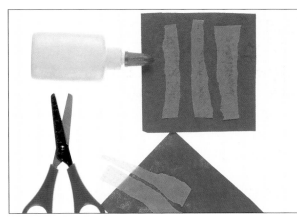

1 Fold a piece of colored paper in half to form the card. Tear off pieces of lime green tissue paper and use small amounts of glue to stick them onto the card.

2 Now layer on strips of pink tissue paper and follow these with a border of blue tissue paper strips. When the glue has set, your card is ready for you to sign and send to a friend.

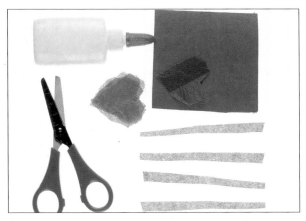

3 This eyecatching Valentine card is easy to make. You will need to layer 4 pieces of red tissue paper together, fold them in half, and carefully tear out a heart shape. The border of the card is made from scissor-cut pieces of red tissue paper.

# Index

ST. COLETTE SCHOOL
ROLLING MEADOWS, ILLINOIS

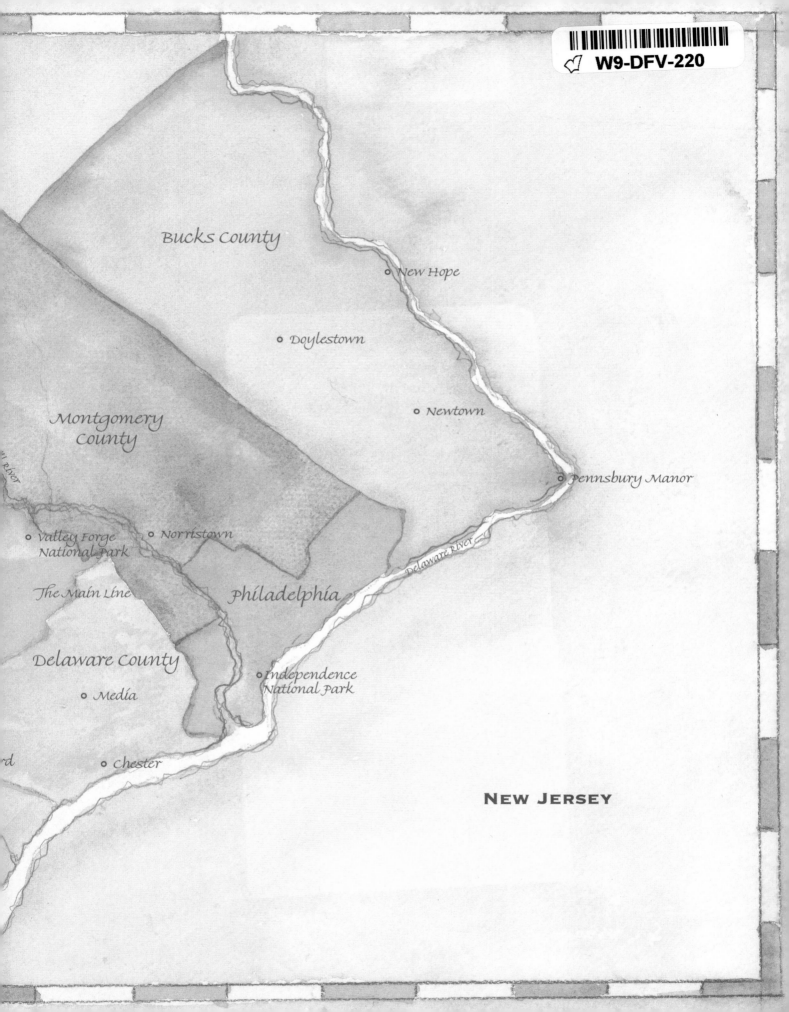

W9-DFV-220

Bucks County

o New Hope

o Doylestown

o Newtown

Montgomery
County

o Pennsbury Manor

*River*

o Valley Forge
National Park

o Norristown

*Delaware River*

The Main Line

Philadelphia

Delaware County

o Independence
National Park

o Media

rd

o Chester

**NEW JERSEY**

BRUMBACK LIBRARY

3 3045 00091 0279

974.8     Seitz, Ruth Hoover.          $29.95
SEI  8/95     Philadelphia &
              its countryside

**THE BRUMBACK LIBRARY**
OF VAN WERT COUNTY
VAN WERT, OHIO

GAYLORD

Philadelphia and Its Countryside
Text © 1994 by Ruth Hoover Seitz
Photography© 1994 by Blair Seitz
ISBN 1-879441-94-2

Library of Congress Catalog Card
Number 94-092129

All rights reserved. No part of this
book may be reproduced or transmitted in any form or by any
means, electronic or mechanical,
including photocopying, recording
or by any information storage or
retrieval system without written
permission from the author, except
for inclusion of brief quotations in
a review.

Published by

RB
BOOKS

Seitz and Seitz, Inc.
1006 N. Second St.
Harrisburg, PA 17102-3121
Designed by V. Green Associates
Printed in Hong Kong

# PHILADELPHIA
## & its Countryside

**RB**
**BOOKS**
HARRISBURG, PA

RUTH HOOVER SEITZ
PHOTOGRAPHY BY BLAIR SEITZ
FOREWORD BY JAMES A. MICHENER

974.8 SE1

# *Foreword*
# BY JAMES A. MICHENER

*Since Philadelphia was our queen city during the building of our nation, where the great documents of our* liberty were forged: the Declaration of Independence and the Constitution, it is appropriate that the city has a circle of jewels enclosing it.

The four counties that touch the city's boundaries, Delaware to the south, Chester to the west, Montgomery to the northwest and Bucks to the northeast, are quiet, often rural areas of marked physical beauty and rare historic charm. Because the Delaware River forms the eastern boundary, with New Jersey on the other side of the river, the four counties define Philadelphia, so far as the Pennsylvania landscape is involved.

And they are jewels, each providing some special contribution to make the area unique, inviting and a major part of early America. First of all, the landscape can be magnificent, in a quiet, rolling way. The mix of hill and valley provided fine vistas and rich land for the early farmers, an interesting blend of families which had been the yeomen of England and Germans who had fled to the New World to find religious freedom. This interlocking of two cultures will be evident throughout the crescent counties.

Second, the architecture surviving from the early days is a fascinating colonial style. Old cottages are tucked away in spots so lovely that modern owners tend to leave both the building and its setting just as they were two centuries ago.

Third, the sprawling Delaware River on the east locks everything together in a compact setting and provides not only a port city for Philadelphia but also beautiful riverside roads in the northern reaches.

Fourth, today the four counties have a chain of interesting towns and villages that delight the tourist and offer a rich mixture of antique shops, some with colonial treasures. A turn around the next corner is apt to provide some surprising vista.

Fifth, religion was always important in the counties. William Penn's Quakers favored simplicity, honest government and good citizenship, but the Germans had a more worldly emphasis, focusing on land ownership, conservative political ideas and family cohesion. The meeting houses of the Quakers are lessons in simplicity, while the churches of the German Mennonites and their attendant sects are structures of stately beauty.

As a longtime resident of the four counties—I lived in Bucks and attended Swarthmore College in Delaware—I recommend two explorations which will give you a taste of what makes the counties so alluring. In Bucks County drive down to the banks of the Delaware River at Washington's Crossing and follow the old coal-barge canal north past New Hope. At times you will ride between the canal on the west and the river on the east, but always you will see beautiful vistas.

Then leave Philadelphia where it touches Montgomery and drive westward through those magnificent towns and villages which comprise what people of the region call our Main Line. Here stand the big gracious homes with their endless lawns, the quaint railway stations, the towns with their famous colleges: the three Quaker schools of major reputation, Bryn Mawr originally for girls, Haverford for boys and Swarthmore, in nearby Delaware County, for both. Not forgetting the excellent Catholic University, Villanova, known locally as 'The Notre Dame of the East.'

The Main Line takes its name from the Pennsylvania Railroad's major roadway between Philadelphia and Chicago, but its local importance is its schedule of commuter trains that bring the suburban residents from Ardmore, Bryn Mawr, Wayne and Paoli into the city.

There we have the four crescent counties that festoon our major city. They are a handsome lot with much to offer.

29.95

# PHILADELPHIA
## & its Countryside

*Europeans who set their sails for Pennsylvania in the 17th century headed towards the watershed of two great rivers, the Delaware and the Schuylkill. These rivers and their tributaries thread through four thriving and scenic counties—Bucks, Chester, Delaware and Montgomery— which crescent Philadelphia, America's fifth largest city.*

# WILLIAM PENN AND HIS VISION

*He was a man ahead of his time. He was a political reformer who promoted religious toleration* and democratic principles while his society imprisoned dissenters. William Penn (1644-1718) stretched the parameters of his heritage as an English aristocrat. Although he was on a first-name basis with royalty, he made arrangements for all classes to settle in his colony, Pennsylvania.

Penn was a 17th century idealist who turned his back on a military career to the disappointment of his admiral father. Penn converted to the Religious Society of Friends, a decision that brought persecution from the Anglican England of his day. In prison, he wrote his beliefs and formulated such advanced ideas as an organization of European states and a union of all the colonies.

But Penn was more than a theorist. In his travels as a Quaker evangelist, he saw the suffering of Friends and other Christians and determined to create a refuge free of laws like the Conventicle Act that punished non-Anglican religious groups that assembled.

Founding a colony based on religious toleration, participatory government and a spirit of brotherly love, William Penn had the inner courage to take this "Holy Experiment" from the dream stage to reality. Penn asked King Charles II for that territory of New World woods lying west of New Jersey and between New York and Maryland. As proprietor, Penn would open his colony to the persecuted. The deal would also benefit the King by erasing his debt of £16,000 sterling to Penn's late father Sir

*"You shall be governed by laws of your own making and live a free and if you will, a sober and industrious people. I shall not usurp the right of any, or oppress his person...."*

*William Penn 1681*

William and secondly, by relieving England of those free-thinking Quakers who were crowding its courts and jails.

With the formalities finished March 4,1681, William Penn became a proprietor of a 45,000-square-mile land grant called Pennsylvania, a name that honored his father and the colony's woodlands. Instead of hurrying to see it, the new proprietor busied himself for 16 months with planning for its government and settlement. Poring over maps, he determined three categories of land ownership and sent out flyers to advertise his "Holy Experiment."

Although Penn made only two trips to Pennsylvania, spending less than four years in his proprietary colony, he left a strong imprint on its structure. It began with his Frame of Government, which ensured a participatory role for freemen in the judicial and executive branches as well as a court system and penal code, which provided that the punishment fit the crime.

Education for all was important to Penn. His Second Frame of Government prescribed "a public school that would be open to all children, rich or poor." Philadelphia's Quakers acted on this directive, establishing the Friends Public School in1689. That school continues today as William Penn Charter School.

But the most important aspect to Penn was religious liberty, "that all persons living in this province who...acknowledge... God to be the creator, and that hold themselves obliged in conscience to live peaceably and justly in civil society, shall in no ways be molested or prejudiced for their religious persuasion... ." In Puritain New England, Quakers were physically tortured and arrested without warrant. Pennsylvania would honor the liberty of conscience.

The Pennsylvania difference was first evident in the colony's settlers. With the Quakers eventually came Mennonites, Amish, Seventh Day Baptists, Schwenkfelders, Moravians and others whose religious practices caused conflict with European governments. They were a hardworking lot. Many wrote letters to their relatives that shared the enthusiasm of one Irish Quaker: "come here, directly, it being the best country for working folk and tradesmen of any in the world... ."

And many did come. By the end of 1685, nearly 90 ships had transported almost 8,000 settlers to Pennsylvania. Penn was pleased with their industry. He praised the linen production of Mennonites in the hamlet of Rittenhouse. Describing the Mennonites as a sober people who will neither fight nor swear, he urged ship captains to "treat them well so more will come over."

Penn dealt more fairly with the Native Americans than any other colonial leader. As a result, his relationship with the Delawares is legendary. Even today, Pennsylvanians entertain an image of a stately, but somewhat portly William Penn in a broad black hat, surrounded by a band of severely-clothed Englishmen presenting gifts to a group of Native Americans.

This popularized exchange originated with the Quaker artist Benjamin West, who painted "Penn's Treaty With the Indians" in 1771, almost a century after Penn arrived. Penn's somber, dark clothes more closely fitted the garb of Quakers during the artist's era than during Penn's time. Penn sported a blue sash and hardly looked so senior at the age of 42.

In reality, there were numerous treaties with Penn paying for the land more than once. After one such purchase, Penn wrote "... great promises passed between us of kindness and good neighborhood, and that the Indians and English must live in love as long as the sun gave light." With no comprehension of exclusive ownership, the Delawares thought they were sharing the land with Europeans.

On two occasions Caleb Pusey, head of a tribunal of "Peace-Makers" who were assigned by Penn to negotiate matters before they came to litigation, handled delicate misunderstandings with tribespeople without force. A close friend of Penn, Pusey was one of the influential Quaker colleagues who bought a grant of more than 5,000 acres. The Pusey cottage, where this family lived in Upland between 1683 and 1717 is still open for guests. Unlike the ubiquitous "George Washington Slept Here,"

this is the only remaining building in America that we know about where Penn spent a night.

His country estate, Pennsbury Manor, is a 1930s reconstruction. Penn's letters directing its building and management reveal the proprietor's interest in horticulture and his love of fine food. The manor's bright fabrics and numerous chairs remind visitors that Penn's lifestyle was a notch above the settlers who dug caves along the river for their first shelter. Today it is possible to observe how Pennsbury may have operated had Penn not departed suddenly to tend such urgent matters as a border dispute with Maryland and financial misunderstandings. Penn's frustration heightened because he was not able to collect cash rents from many settlers in Pennsylvania.

In Penn's absence, the influence of his ideals lessened. Disagreements tarnished provincial peace even though the Quaker majority in the provincial council supported Penn's policy of no standing army. Not surprisingly, Quakers are proud to take credit for the lavish clock tower on the State House because such expenditures reduced the amount of money in the provincial coffers for war debts.

Although many Americans associate the Liberty Bell with our independence story, our greatest symbol of liberty actually exists because of William Penn. It was cast to commemorate the 50th anniversary of Penn's Charter of Privileges, the democratic constitution that the founder granted his colonists in 1701. The bell cracked upon arrival in 1752. It was recast and hung in the State House tower. Its title came when anti-slavery groups attached its inscription, "Proclaim liberty," to their cause.

Today people around the world honor this talisman of freedom; they come to Philadelphia to see and touch it. Its Biblical words, "Proclaim liberty 'thro all the land to all the inhabitants thereof—" remind all of the freedom and privileges extended to settlers in Penn's colony.

*Left* Built between 1684 and 1699 as a country retreat for William Penn, Pennsbury Manor was reconstructed in the 1930s on its original Bucks County site. *Center* The Morton Homestead in Prospect Park is an example of the log homes built by Swedes and Finns, the first European settlers in Pennsylvania. Their expeditions began in 1638, preceding William Penn by several decades. *Right* The Brinton1704 house in Chester County exhibits the medieval English lifestyle of early well-to-do Quaker settlers who accepted Penn's invitation.

*Top Left* Pennsbury Manor along the Delaware River is the only residence of William Penn, in Britain or America, that is open to the public. *Left* With gables, shutters and a porch, Buckingham Friends Meetinghouse, built in 1768, is typical of Quaker places of worship. *Above* The lead statue of Wm. Penn, made by Englishman John Bacon in the 1760s, has stood in front of Pennsylvania Hospital since Penn's grandson, John, donated it in 1804.

# AN ARENA FOR BUILDING A NATION

*Beginnings always deserve commemoration. And creating a nation is a huge beginning.*

No other area of America offers as much about our national start up as Philadelphia and the four counties that rim it. Near residential developments with such names as Freedoms View Estates, Liberty Knoll and Independence Place, are battle sites where British redcoats and poorly equipped revolutionaries tangled in combat between 1775 and 1778.

In Philadelphia's Old City, Independence National Historical Park squares off America's most historic mile. It encompasses at least two dozen sites marking where nationhood evolved from complaint letters to a declaration of independence and finally, a constitution with balanced power. There are well-restored brick structures, areas of shaded grass and such realisms as hitching posts and boxes for the city watch. One of the park's few modern buildings, the visitor center on 3rd Street, orients many of its five million annual visitors. By carriage or foot, they then venture into layers of 18th century events with the help of a map or a guide.

A favorite stop is Independence Hall, which was the Pennsylvania State House in colonial days. The most striking endeavor in creating a nation took place here 11 years after Independence. Americans were no longer British subjects. The thirteen colonies were now states extending from the forests of Maine almost to the Gulf of Mexico and westward from the Atlantic Ocean to the Mississippi. No other country had tried to set up a republican form of

*"oppression makes a poor country, and a desperate people, who always wait an opportunity to change."*

*William Penn*

government stretching over such an expansive area. Honing these states into a government that could run an independent nation was the work of 55 delegates to the Constitutional Convention. In May, 1787, they met in the Assembly Room, our country's most historic political meeting place. It was a familiar setting to those who had been here in mid-1776 to adopt the Declaration of Independence or to ratify the Articles of Confederation in 1781.

Day after day, the delegates proposed, debated and compromised. The talk was often as heated as the room. But by early August the Convention had framed a structure for the people to enact and enforce laws. Power would be balanced among three branches of government. Taxes and tariffs would be levied. Commerce would be regulated. The preamble summarized the provisions of a government run by "We, the People... ."

David Dutcher, the park's historian, credits their success to their like-mindedness. "The founding fathers had gone to the same schools, had studied the theories of Locke, Hume and Montesquieu. Many were even related."

What groundbreakers they were, putting a republic into practice. Knowing that there was no such government in the world, George Washington admitted, "I stand on untrodden ground!" Benjamin Franklin thought their government might last 50 years. James Madison would only give it 20 or 30. Wouldn't all those nation builders be confounded that their plan for governing is still in place, with power transferred peacefully several dozen times over the last two centuries?

The whole process began because the colonists didn't want to pay taxes when they had no representatives in the British Parliament. Disgruntled delegates from every colony except Georgia had met at Carpenter's Hall in 1773 and drafted a request for justice to the mother country. Despite the sweltering heat, the doors and windows had remained closed so that none of the representatives of the Crown could overhear their plans. In response, King George III heaped more taxes on his Colonies, a population of 2.6 million people, and two years later, they protested by signing a document of severance, the Declaration of Independence.

When the document was read aloud July 8, 1775, on the grounds of the Pennsylvania State House, Philadelphians cheered; drums rolled and bells rang. John Adams wrote prophetically that this event would be "the most memorable in American history, celebrated by succeeding generations from one end of the continent to the other from this time forward forevermore." Americans were free!

Independence Day or America's birthday is on July 4, the date that Congress adopted the Declaration of Independence, a brilliant political statement written by Thomas Jefferson in just 17 days. The setting where he penned it, the Graff House at 7th and Market Streets, has been reconstructed for touring.

The revolutionaries had to fight for the freedom that they had declared. In an act punishable by death, some militiamen tore down the King's coat of arms and set it afire. The revolt was on. After the Second Continental Congress "totally dissolved political connection between... these united colonies... and the state of Great Britain," it reconvened in the Assembly Room at the State House and authorized modest George Washington to command the patriot forces. While General Washington mustered troops and faced the British in the northern colonies, the colony's delegates wrestled with issues of war and finances in the State House, now Independence Hall.

Soliciting aid from France was the focus of a very dedicated Philadelphian, Benjamin Franklin. His diplomatic success brought much-needed funds in 1777 at the end of the troops' encampment at Valley Forge. While they wintered on this rise on the other side of the Schuylkill, the British occupied Philadelphia. "A most filthy and sordid situation" resulted from their quartering troops in the State House.

The Continental troops who were hunkered down at Valley Forge may have viewed their own plight as similar. Their rations were as irregular as their support from the Congress. The mud huts that they built for themselves were probably more makeshift than the ones on site today at Valley Forge Park.

Visitors roam over the park's 3,000 acres by car, bicycle or foot. A visitor center and markers interpret what thousands of soldiers endured there in 1777-78.

Another park farther north and along the Delaware River honors an earlier episode in the Continental Army's fight for freedom. In 1776, Washington's troops lost several New York skirmishes. By Christmas the British were entrenched for the winter with Washington's dispirited forces in safe but shabby retreat on the Pennsylvania side of the river.

At an inn near McConkey's Ferry, Washington finalized a bold offensive. On Christmas Day he would surprise the Hessians, German mercenaries who were defending New Jersey for the Crown. Fighting brutal gusts, he and his troops transported their supplies and 18 cannon on boats that were used to haul iron ore. An island hid their launch from enemy view. The Bucks County site of this courageous maneuver is now called Washington Crossing Historic Park.

Every December 25, reenactors dressed like Washington and his troops walk from the 1752 Inn at the ferry crossing to the shore and row Durham boats — eight oarsmen apiece — across the Delaware, reliving the drama of that wintry night. The thousands who observe from the village, which is still very 18th century, remember that Washington's strategy paid off. The Continental Army had two wins in New Jersey. Washington's decisiveness gave his disheartened soldiers a needed boost of confidence.

Washington Crossing Historic Park includes 500 acres with dwellings that were significant in General Washington's successful plan. Besides housing General Washington, the Inn at McConkey's Ferry was a guardpost for the Continental Army. The Thompson-Neely House is furnished as it may have been as the headquarters of Major General Lord Stirling who was in charge of the troops along the Delaware. Sheep bleat in the farmyard of the restored stone barn. The family's reconstructed mill is at the site where soldiers got "raw flour" to appease their hunger more than two centuries ago. A hike to the top of Bowman's Hill offers the view that convinced Stirling that the daring crossing could succeed.

As Washington moved his troops, he encountered mixed views of the revolution. Loyalists preferred to remain under British royalty and profited by selling supplies to the redcoats for hard cash. Sympathetic farm families—like the Thompsons north of McConkey's

Ferry and the Rings and Gilpins near the Brandywine River—evacuated so Washington and his generals could rent their homes for military planning. In keeping with their support of peace, some Quakers remained neutral.

This was probably the mindset of Elizabeth Chads, a Chester County Quaker widow whose farm became a battlefield on September 11, 1777. During the Battle of Brandywine, one regiment of patriots took cover below the hill where her husband, John, a ferry operator at Chadds Ford, had built a stone house c.1725.

Widow Chads and her farm survived. Her diary recounts no losses to "the Mansion," as neighbors referred to her house, luxuriously endowed with scarce glass windows. Visitors often enjoyed tea—with spoons provided—in Elizabeth's main parlor. It was more typical in this rural area for visitors to bring their own silverware. As troops poured into her valley, Elizabeth continued with her duties, but thrust her precious silver spoons in the pockets that she tied around her waist each morning.

Many other residents suffered heavily. Twenty-six thousand soldiers trampled fields and fired shot of various sizes over a 10-square-mile area. Those who assisted the rebels, such as Gideon Gilpin, a middle-class Quaker farmer who provided lodging to Marquis de General Lafayette, Washington's new aide, were plundered by the victorious British troops. A tour of Gilpin's restored farmstead and the visitor center at The Brandywine Battlefield Park on Route 1 sheds light on that day's events.

A stop by the John Chads House along Route 100 reveals Elizabeth's lifestyle as a well-cared for widow. On the climb up the hill from the springhouse, you may catch a whiff of ginger mingled with wood smoke

Many weekends, interpreter Lise Taylor fires the beehive oven, tests its temperature with her bare arm and is able to bake the gamut from crusty bread to scones for hours after she has removed the fuel.

John Chads was innovative in attaching the oven to the house and in making a candle niche in the walk-in hearth. The hundreds of loaves that still come out of Elizabeth's oven each year provide visitors to this house museum with a slice of her life and also finance activities of the Chadds Ford Historical Society.

Behind every open-to-the-public historic site is such a support group. Thousands of volunteers in the Delaware Valley raise funds, organize festivals and offer tours and living history experiences to keep buildings, museums and monuments a part of Americans' heritage.

The Independence story stays alive at events such as the October reenactment of the patriots' defeat at the Battle of Germantown in 1777 at Cliveden, a summer mansion six miles north of Philadelphia. Visits to the Betsy Ross House in Philadelphia, and to Paoli's Waynesborough, the home of General Anthony Wayne (1745-96), who fought in almost every Revolutionary War battle, pinpoint the contributions of individual freedom fighters. Many Americans return more than once to the Liberty Bell, a national symbol of freedom, which has remained in view 24 hours a day since the U.S. Bicentennial in 1976. Here in southeastern Pennsylvania, where America birthed a nation, history has always had a glow that keeps past beginnings bright for the next generation.

*Right* Shown here is a detail of the 21' x 12' copy of Emanuel Leutze's oil painting, "Washington Crossing the Delaware" which hangs at Washington Crossing Historic Park.

*Top Left* At Valley Forge, General George Washington's wintering troops built huts, now restored at the Park's Muhlenberg's Brigade. *Left* At a Battle of Germantown reenactment, British soldiers and Hessians fight against the patriots. *Above* Colonial iron-making influenced the Revolutionary War. At Dilworthtown's Arden Forge, which was built by James Dilworth in 1745, Peter A. Renzetti uses 18th century iron-making techniques. *Above Right* During the Battle of Brandywine, Lafayette, Washington's aide, occupied the home of Quaker Gideon Gilpin.

*Top Left* At a Valley Forge reenactment, Emily Breslin and James Trainor cook in the manner of the revolutionaries. *Bottom* The John Chads House on a hill above the Brandywine River interprets 18th century life in the hamlet of Chadds Ford. *Above Left* Philadelphia's Independence Hall (1732-48) is the site of the signing of the Declaration of Independence and the adoption of the Constitution. *Above Right* Period spectacles, case, quill pen, ballot box and pipe adorn a table in the Hall's Assembly Room.

# PHILADELPHIA,
## a "Greene Countrie Towne"

*No city celebrates America's birthday like Philadelphia, her fifth largest metropolis.*

Each July 4, the fervor starts in Independence Historical National Park where the first celebration erupted in 1776. Political leaders speak in front of Independence Hall, and since 1988, the Philadelphia Liberty Medal with cash award of $100,000 is presented to a person or organization from anywhere in the world that "has led in the pursuit of freedom from oppression." Fife and drum corps play in 18th century attire and flags with a circle of 13 stars billow in the summer breeze.

The Independence Day parade features color guard drills, high school bands and ethnic dance groups. Brilliantly costumed groups march downtown and then west between the national flags hanging along the Ben Franklin Parkway. Crowds enthusiastically cheer the marchers approaching the final leg at Eakins Oval. People on the sidelines sip strawberry smoothies and tear into soft pretzels.

By dusk, thousands have staked a claim on the art museum lawn, but more keep pouring in until over a million people settle down for an evening concert and fireworks. Excitement builds with balloons and glow sticks. Various languages waft across the crowd. Rousing cheers and dancing break out with the music. The fireworks are well worth the wait. Brilliant showers of light burst over the museum roof. In the finale, they light up to the beat of the music. It's America's birthday in the city where its nationhood was born. Happy Independence!

*"And thou, Philadelphia, the virgin settlement of this province named before thou wert born. what love, what care, what service and what travail have there been to bring thee forth.... My soul prays to God for thee..."*

*William Penn*

Next day, the squirrels in Independence Square are at play, just as they were when they amused the philosopher Henry David Thoreau during his 1854 visit. Philadelphians and visitors seek shade under trees lining the pavement. Center city workers relax near the hot-red LOVE sculpture at Kennedy Plaza over their noontime break. Others scoot into Wanamaker's, the department store that was the first to offer fixed prices and a restaurant. The store's historic organ entertains shoppers daily and is as much a symbol of this retail flagship as its bronze eagle, a common meeting place in the Grand Court.

Benjamin Franklin claimed that Philadelphia was so beautiful and orderly a city that it would convince an atheist that there was a God. This exaggeration reveals the hometown pride of a citizen who was very familiar with European cities. In reality, Philadelphia was planned to be better than London, where narrow streets and dense frame housing had fueled a devastating fire in 1666. William Penn directed Surveyor-General Thomas Holme to lay out his "Greene Countrie Towne" with parallel and straight streets and two wider avenues crossing in the middle.

The city's grid design is obvious from the William Penn statue atop City Hall. From a platform just below Penn's shoes, viewers immediately spot one of the longest, straightest streets in America, Broad Street, which is a substitution for 14th Street in the lineup of north-south numbered streets.

In clear view are the corporate towers that broke an unwritten law by rising above Penn's statue in the 1980s, pushing Philadelphia's skyline into the 20th century. During the Depression, the PSFS Building went up as America's first glass-sleek skyscraper of the international style. Over three decades the Penn Center Complex integrated offices, retail stores and public transportation around a pedestrian concourse. Besides restoring old charmers like Lit Brothers Store and The Bourse for new uses, the city realized new meccas such as The Gallery, a dramatic four-level mall, One Liberty Place and its sequel with their stunning facades and a downtown Convention Center. Designed for service and beauty, its 1.3 million square feet are all the more valuable for their under-roof access by train and airport shuttle.

With much construction and restoration completed over the last two decades, Philadelphia faces its greatest challenge in City Hall, the finest example of Second Empire architecture. What was unusual and ornate in the late 1800s is an albatross for climate control and telecommunications today. Its artistic interior flashed onto 1993 movie screens in the courtroom scene in *Philadelphia* and merits a tour.

Manufacturing figured heavily into Philadelphia's growth throughout the first half of the 20th century. Consumers were already aware of Stetson hats, Vici gloves and Hires root beer. Baldwin locomotives were shipped throughout the world, and Yellin wrought ironwork for estates and public buildings. Although almost half of the area's employees at the end of World War II depended on the manufacturing sector, by the eighties only 12 percent of the total work force headed for factories each day. Construction and service industries picked up some of the flack. For instance, in the Old City, a baby carriage factory is now a superb inn. A sugar refinery is an apartment complex. Society Hill sleekness replaced the city's food distribution center near Dock Street. With coins still in demand, the United States Mint at 7th and Arch Streets strikes almost 2 million quarters and 20 million pennies each day.

The Delaware River Port Authority oversees one of the busiest international ports along the North Atlantic. Terminals stretch along a 15-mile shoreline from north of the city to Chester. Philadelphia is a major entry point for U.S. and Canada's winter supply of fruits from Chile. Seven refineries along the Delaware make Philadelphia the East's biggest processor of oil products.

As the nation's birthplace, Philadelphia is bound to be a city of American firsts. A city planned by its founder for free-thinkers who longed to be self-governing, Philadelphia attracted enterprising settlers. It is no wonder that the first paper mill was in production by 1690, when the city totaled 600 homes. America's first magazine was published here, and several decades later, its first daily newspaper. In the area of business, Philadelphia birthed the first insurance company, the first trust company, the first bank and the first building and loan company.

In the medical capital of the world, Philadelphia's health institutions also clasp a handful of firsts in America. The first women's medical college. The first medical school (now there are six in the city). In 1751, the first hospital. The first dispensary.

This city is home to America's oldest zoo, which holds a lineup of landmark records in zoodom. In the late 19th century it housed the first adult male elephant in the country. In 1993 the zoo welcomed the first white lions for exhibit in this hemisphere. Zoo animals around the globe enjoy zoocake, a nutritional dish developed in the Philly zoo's kitchen.

Self-improvement for the improvement of the community was a motto of one of Philadelphia's most inventive and charming citizens, Benjamin Franklin (1706-1790). His resourcefulness gave society many labor-saving gadgets and equipped his city with police and fire departments. Self-taught, he founded America's first subscription library in 1731, now the Library Company of Philadelphia with more than 300,000 volumes including such treasures as the guidebook for Lewis and Clark's 1804 expedition. From 1744, Franklin brought together scientists organized as the American Philosophical Society. The illustrious University of Pennsylvania developed from the Academy for the Education of Youth, which was founded by Franklin to be the most liberal of schools of higher learning in the colonies.

Young Philadelphia was a venue for trying new approaches, especially in governing. Dave Dutcher, Independence Park's historian, notes that our national leaders cut their teeth in Philadelphia. "The first nine presidents were in Philadelphia between 1775 and 1800 in some governmental capacity."

Those leaders heralded British tradition, but Philadelphia now presents a diversity that might even surprise its egalitarian founder, Penn. The summer festivals at Penn's Landing are proof. Poles, Italians, Irish, Latinos, Indians and African-Americans showcase their music, dance and foods, often in costume, at the Delaware waterfront.

On a sunny August weekend, Polish folks in red and

white parade their heritage. Booths display Polish love knots and T-shirts emblazoned with "Polish and Proud."

The food stands hark back to the old country. Church-women sell pastries such as Polish donuts filled with plum jelly. While some people line up for *kielbasa,* a succulent sausage, others go for *pierogies,* dough pyramids stuffed with potatoes and *sauerkraut.* A jovial nun in a white habit turns *placki,* potato pancakes that fry to a crisp. Polka music blares from the Stephen Girard Pavilion. As the crowd swells, people squeeze onto the steps facing the river where pleasure boats cruise. They cheer the dancers who swing to songs from various regions of Poland. Strong accordion rhythms carry their feet into fast kicks, high jumps and hoists high on the shoulder. An ethnic festival is a time to be who you are and to whoop it up being that.

With almost 40 percent of Philadelphia's population African-American, there are more than a dozen black culture festivals each year. Unity Day is the centerpiece. Each third Sunday in August, 800,000 people stream onto the Ben Franklin Parkway for a family-oriented festival sponsored since 1978 by WDAS radio station. Between Logan Circle and Eakins Oval, folks take in performances on six stages and enjoy activities that are targeted for all, kiddies to seniors.

African-Americans from the region also gather each July for a two-day Black Family Reunion near Memorial Hall in Fairmount Park. The celebration features "edu-tainment" in tented program areas. Panels, workshops and performances lure attendees into a range of self-improvement areas. Rhythm and blues and gospel concerts finish off the highly participatory days.

During ODUNDE in June, African music, fashions and artifacts pour onto South Street. On this one-day event, which means Happy New Year in Yoruba, blacks enjoy Afrocentric merrymaking.

Joviality also struts along Philadelphia's streets in winter. There is nothing like the Mummers Parade,

Pennsylvania's own Mardi Gras. It begins early New Year's Day with lavishly masqueraded marchers lining up in South Philadelphia and heading up Broad Street to perform for the judges at City Hall. The raucous jokes, the colorful and outlandish costumes and the high-steppin' music cast doubt on H. L. Mencken's description of Philadelphia as "the most pecksniffian of American cities." The Baltimore writer did not take into consideration that many other flavors entered Philly's port along with Quaker sobriety. The Swedes, Greeks, Italians and British each contributed to the fanfare that sparked the parade in 1901. But what the Philadelphia New Year Shooters and Mummers Association masterminds is a true Philly phenomenon.

At least 47 clubs prepare all year long to enter one of the four divisions — comics, fancies, string bands and fancy brigades. Among the thousands parading the 2.5-mile route are comics tossing out satirical remarks and entrants in the Fancy Club dazzling the crowd as rainbow-colored characters. The presentations of the string bands are real crowd-pleasers. Near the end of the 12-hour extravaganza come the brigades who depict a theme in elaborate costumes.

Over the years songs have been written for the Mummers Parade that rose in the national charts. One that is still frequently heard in a parade medley is "Oh, Dem Golden Slippers." The simple tune matches the mummers' strut, and don't dare call it a march.

Fundraising by the clubs, many located on Second Street near the Mummers Museum, pays for costumes, music and props. The group spirit that feeds this phantasmagoria was bred in Philadelphia's neighborhoods where belonging still counts.

Philadelphia handles its diversity by being a city of neighborhoods. Novelist Henry James called them "human groups that discriminate in their own favor." Neighbors of the same ethnicity may live in a section with similar houses and go to the same churches, activities and stores. This allegiance may hold for several generations.

No matter where you live, you know where to get the best cheesesteaks, Philadelphia's own sandwich. In West Philadelphia it may be Larry's, which advertised "Best Cheesesteaks in the World" until it added hoagies and became "Home of the Belly Fillers since 1956." Whether you buy them at Jim's, Geno's or Pat's, you need to understand cheesesteak protocol. This South Philly original—thinly sliced beef grilled and bedded into an Italian roll with fried onions, sauce and cheese—is best eaten outside and on the spot. Leaning on a dumpster to devour its oozing richness may further improve the taste.

Frankie Olivieri, Jr., owner of Pat's, says that the sandwich idea came from his grandfather quite by accident in 1930. To vary his own lunch, Harry threw some chopped beef on the outdoor grill where he made hot dogs to sell. A cab driver drove up and insisted on buying whatever was cooking. Harry reluctantly handed over his lunch, and the cabby returned raving about the sandwich. The steak sandwich soon became their staple with cheese added in the fifties.

Some cheesesteaks find their way into the stomachs of presidents and movie stars, but 60 percent of the customers who queue up at Pat's and across the street at Geno's come from this Italian neighborhood where families have lived all their lives and understand each other's dramatic verbal shorthand.

Six blocks away at Ninth Street, the Italian Market is its busiest on Saturday morning. Its bustle and its offerings—fresh pasta, long sausages, mounds of vegetables and crusty bread right out of the oven—are the same as they were a half century ago. Back then, the stallholders were immigrants from Italy; now many are transplants from Asia.

In South Philadelphia, very near Interstate 95, stands the Gloria Dei Church, which was built by the Swedes who settled here 40 years before Penn arrived. The remains of a lightning rod on the brick exterior are a reminder that the last rector from Sweden, Nils Collin, was a good friend of Ben Franklin who invented this safety device.

A jag to the northwest is Mother Bethel A.M.E. Church, a beautiful structure on the oldest parcel of real estate that has been continuously owned by blacks. Here, a denomination of four million emerged from a self-help movement, the Free African Society, which was organized by Richard Allen (1760-1831) and Absalom Jones (1746-1818) at the time of the Constitutional Convention in 1787.

Both men bought themselves out of slavery and became lay preachers at Old St. George's, the first Methodist Church in Philadelphia. On one historic occasion, the church hierarchy asked a group gathered under their leadership at the 5:00 a.m. service to go to the gallery. The response of this largely black group was the first non-violent protest of discrimination in America. They asked to finish their prayer and agreed to leave. In his autobiography Allen wrote, "They were no more plagued by us."

Allen and his followers hauled a blacksmith shop to the present site and founded the African Methodist Episcopal Church where all could worship.

During the yellow fever epidemic in1793, he and his members assisted the respected Dr. Benjamin Rush and helped to bury some of the 4,000 Philadelphians who died. During that grave era, some residents fled to Germantown, a settlement six miles north that was high enough to be a reprieve from heat and disease. President George Washington and his family rented a summer residence that is now on exhibit by Independence National Historical Park as the Deshler-Morris House. He held four cabinet meetings here.

Today Germantown is a unique city mix of historic dwellings, patches of greenery, food takeouts and struggling housing. Its market brings together Amish stallholders from Lancaster, African-American neighbors and Asian vendors.

When Germans first settled here in 1683, they built houses on both sides of a Native American trail and excelled at linen and paper production. That trail is now Germantown Avenue with a cobblestone stretch to remind everyone of its historic past. A variety of buildings, many on this national landmark road, invite the public into the lives of adventuresome settlers of the past two centuries.

Each fall, visitors return to Cliveden, the Georgian country home of Benjamin Chew, for a reenactment of the Battle of Germantown. As chief justice of the supreme court of Pennsylvania, Chew favored negotiation with the British above revolution. He was under house arrest in New Jersey when the British closed the shutters and made his house a fortress against the advancing patriots. Washington's troops could not penetrate the thick walls and lost the battle.

Upon return, Chew found his spacious house "an

absolute wreck." Since then, six more generations of Chews lived in the house and today 75 percent of the treasures in this house museum were passed on through the family.

Flush with Germantown Avenue is the Johnson House, one of the rare sites that is known to be part of the Underground Railroad, a secretive network of concerned persons who assisted slaves to gain freedom. According to a granddaughter of Samuel and Jennett Johnson, in the mid-1800s an estimated 600 slaves passed through this Quaker home over an 11-year period. The activities of their 11 children, a front office for the tannery in the rear, and domestic employees served to conceal any additional people. Germantown was one day's walk from two slaveholding states, Maryland and Delaware, and this house was one of the pivotal stopovers for fleeing slaves.

The northernmost suburbs, Mt. Airy and Chestnut Hill, have been solid communities since families first claimed them as ideal residential turf in the railroad era. "Hillers" benefit from clusters of unique shops (85 percent individually owned), superb schools and summer concerts in Pastorius Park. They enjoy life that is rich with urban culture and country pleasures.

Philadelphia is large enough to support small museums built around specific interests or the homes of the famous. The Mutter Museum is a quaint collection of 19th century medical items, appropriate for a city that has been on the threshold of medicine. A stop at the house at the corner of Seventh & Spring Garden Streets leads to Edgar Allan Poe's residence during the six most productive years of his life. After a visit to the Philadelphia Maritime Museum, the port of Philadelphia will no longer be an enigma. "Footwear Through the Ages" is featured at the Shoe Museum at the Pennsylvania College of Podiatric Medicine. There are dozens more that amuse and inform. In fact, Philadelphia even has a museum about herself, the Atwater Kent Museum. Its rich historical and archeological collections trace how life was and is in the City of Brotherly Love.

South Street-Headhouse is an 11-block enclave of nightlife. The storefronts throb with color and the wares inside are unique. Even their names are esoteric. Your imagination can go wild at boutiques with outfits from other continents and art-to-wear jewelry.

Then there are more than 80 restaurants, theatres and nightclubs. The eateries fit any mood. Frozen drinks, water ice and specialty desserts can cool down a summer night. For solid fare, Greek, Thai, Creole and Northern Italian are only a few of the cuisine choices. And here, in the most culturally integrated district of Philly, there are delis and bistros with a range of late-night tastes. Having saved itself from a crosstown expressway in the eighties, South Street-Headhouse, an area that has made bohemian classy, celebrates constantly. Besides tourists and students, the celebrants live in nearby Society Hill and Queen's Village, where colonial is chic.

Philadelphia's palm overflows with more than three centuries' worth of accolades. And she's still a city breaking new ground and polishing her historical past. Her 5.5 million residents celebrate being on the cutting edge then and now.

*Right* Independence Hall is the most visited building in Philadelphia's Old City.

*Above* An Independence Day parade streams down the Benjamin Franklin Parkway from City Hall. *Top Left* An Independence Day concert typically precedes the annual fireworks. *Top Right* Speeches in front of Independence Hall along Chestnut Street spark America's birthday celebrations. *Bottom* Philadelphia's former basketball player Julius Erving pumps hands along the parade route.

*Top Left* South Street's festivals pour color and music into this bohemian shopping and eating mecca stretching between 2nd and 7th Sts. *Bottom* A stop at a Chestnut Street sidewalk fortuneteller enlivens the walk to Penn's Landing. *Above* Restored townhouses and horse-drawn carriages keep the 18th and 19th centuries prominent in Society Hill, south of Independence National Park. Originally a Penn grant to the Society of Free Traders, the area bustled with trade until urban renewal successfully changed its face by the 1960s.

*Previous Pages* Viewed from Spring Garden Bridge, multi-lane highways loop to the north and west of Philadelphia's skyline. *Above* Looking east, Market Street, one of the wider avenues planned by William Penn, is a ribbon of commerce. *Top Right* The Chestnut Street Transitway, a one-way route for bus traffic only during the day, streams past stores, restaurants and specialty shops. *Bottom* In the first quarter of the 20th century, the Curtis Building (6th & Walnut Sts.) was the birthplace of the *Ladies' Home Journal* and the *Saturday Evening Post.*

*Left* Public art abounds in Philadelphia, the country's fifth largest city. "The Clothespin" is a 45-foot steel sculpture by Claes Oldenburg on Centre Square Plaza in the shade of City Hall. *Above* More than 250 sculptures grace the exterior of City Hall. Inside, its rooms such as City Council chambers, have ornate features.

*Above* The Philadelphia Museum of Art, built in Greco-Roman architectural style, rests on a hill "Faire Mount" facing the Ben Franklin Parkway. *Top Left* Renaissance Hall, with its circular skylight and relief designs, is one of the splendid rooms in the Masonic Temple on N. Broad St. *Top Right* A Ben Franklin marble sculpture by James Earle Fraser invites the visitors into the Frankin Institute Science Museum. *Bottom* The restored 30th Street Station (1929-34) is the hub of the city's rail transportation.

*Top Left* With charm, Philadelphia meshes heritage with the modern. *Bottom* Once the Lit Brothers Store, Market Place East, a retail complex on Market St., is the only complete block of commercial Victorian architecture in the city. *Center & Above* Completed in 1994, the Pennsylvania Convention Center in Center City includes the renovated Reading Terminal Train Shed. Such design features as 37,000 square yards of custom wool carpet make its multi-functional space pleasing.

*Above* Benjamin Franklin appears at the Pavilion along Independence Mall where visitors touch the 2,080-pound Liberty Bell. *Center* T-shirts for sale honor Philly's professional baseball and football teams, the Phillies and the Eagles. *Top Right* Carriage rides with tour guides explain the historical attractions from Penn's Landing to Washington Square. *Bottom* At the Polish Festival the PKM Dancers perform at Penn's Landing, the site of nearly a hundred concerts and special events between May and September.

*Previous Pages* Awaiting Independence Day fireworks, boats anchor on the Schuylkill near Boathouse Row. *Left* Alexander "Sandy" Calder sculpted "Jerusalem Stabile" (1979), a landmark on the University of Pennsylvania campus. *Center* Enquiring young students experience the Mandell Futures Center at the Franklin Institute Science Museum. *Right* With hands-on activities, the Please Touch Museum attracts children, ages 1-7.

*Top Left* The view north from southwest Philly shows the Schuylkill River and the buildings that create the city skyline. *Bottom* Shops and restaurants opened in 1981 in the restored Bourse, an elaborate merchants exchange (1893-95) that had closed during the Depression. The red sandstone structure is on S. 5th near Independence Mall. *Above* The Gallery is a four-story glass-roofed shopping mall with fountains, a SEPTA train stop and ethnic eateries.

*Above* Rittenhouse Square, one of the four eight-acre parks in Wm. Penn's original city plan, is surrounded by luxury condominiums and blocks of Victorian residences. In the distance rises 60-story One Liberty Place, the first skyscraper to rise higher than the top of Penn's statue on City Hall. *Right* From the Delaware River, the City of Brotherly Love stretches west.

*Previous Pages* Philadelphia's newest skyscrapers— (L to R) Mellon Bank Center, One Liberty Place, Two Liberty Place and Blue Cross Tower—catch the day's last sun. *Above* Each New Year's Day the Mummers Parade struts north on Broad Street mesmerizing the crowd and TV audience. This phantasmagoric show features string bands, comics, fancies and fancy brigades—many with face paint and elaborate costumes decorated with feathers, sequins, braid, ribbon and ruffles. The parade's playful gaudiness is an apt antidote to Philly's gray winters.

*Above* Looking south, this view of the Delaware River encompasses the downtown and northeast Philadelphia. *Top Left* From the Museum of Art, the Ben Franklin Parkway leads to Center City. *Top Right* From atop City Hall on Center Square, this view features W. Market St. and its highrises. *Bottom* Within Independence National Historical Park, this ghost frame within Franklin Court is built over the foundation of Benjamin Franklin's house.

*Above* Covering 37 acres, Penn's Landing is a marina with recreational space along the Delaware — the city site where settlers first disembarked. *Center* A mural by Wm Freeman is an example of the art endeavors of the Philadelphia Anti-Graffiti Network. *Right* Students learn dance at the University of the Arts.

BLACK SMITH SHOP 1791
ROUGHCAST 1805
1ST CHURCH
2ND CHURCH
CHURCH AFRICAN
RICHARD ALLEN
FOUNDER
1760 - 1831
EPISCOPAL METHODIST
4TH CHURCH
3RD CHURCH
AT PRESENT 1889
MOTHER BETHEL
BRICK CHURCH 1841

*Previous Pages* The Senate Chamber in Congress Hall is restored as it was when America's first representatives convened here. *Top Left* Mother Bethel A.M.E. Church, S. 6th St., is the parent church of a denomination of 5 million. *Above* Its founder, Richard Allen (1760-1831), who also organized the first black fraternal order in the city, is buried in the church. *Bottom* At the historic Betsy Ross House, exhibits depict 18th century craftsmanship, including upholstery making.

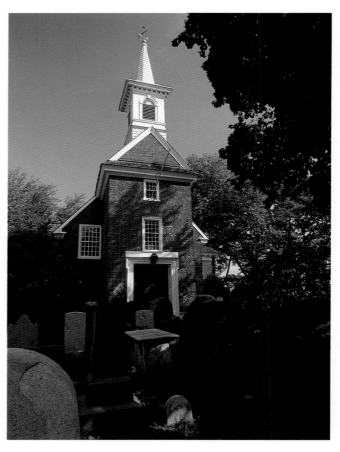

*Top Left* Built of brick by British masons hired by Swedes, Gloria Dei (1698-1700) is the oldest church in the city. *Left* Philadelphians John and Chris Lennon Naulty marry at Cliveden, site of the Revolutionary War's Battle of Germantown. *Above Left* Independence Day fireworks explode above the roof of the art museum. *Above Right* Built in 1926, the Benjamin Franklin Bridge runs from Center City to Camden, spanning the Delaware.

# THE ARTS, FINE AND PRACTICAL

*The November light lies pure across a tawny Chester County field that curves into a hollow.*

In the bottomlands, frost stiffens and beautifies the weeds along a fencerow painted in a dozen earth tones. Walnut and poplar trees stand as mature silhouettes. A few winter birds cavort in the clear light and strong shadows that have been immortalized in tempera by Andrew Wyeth (b. 1917), now world-renowned for his painting. His father, N.C. Wyeth (1882-1945), was his sole teacher. But N.C., who honored imagination throughout his life, did his offspring the favor of rearing them in Chadds Ford, where his own teacher, master illustrator Howard Pyle (1853-1911), had held summer classes. Here, from boyhood, Andrew learned to love the rural earthiness that is in "Spring Fed" and "Distant Thunder." In his neighbors and their land, Andrew found subjects that he could easily endow with unusual perspective and universal themes.

Today visitors can see many of the Wyeths' works at the Brandywine River Museum, a center for artistic study along the banks of its namesake. At the gallery entrance hangs "Portrait of a Pig" by Andrew's son Jamie (b.1946), also an artist of stature. Among his repertoire are still lifes that seem elevated to portraiture. Some of his paintings were inspired by experiences on his farm near Chadds Ford.

The Wyeths were not the only artists to treasure the inspirational scenery of the Delaware Valley. At the turn of the century, Edward W. Redfield (1869-1965), William Lathrop (1859-1938), Daniel Garber (1880-1958) and several

*"Art is good where it is beneficial."*

*William Penn*

other artists located near the Delaware and painted the landscapes of Bucks County. As artists in the "Pennsylvania School of Landscape Painting," they were wooed by the area's rolling hills, stone barns, winding streams and thickets of hardwoods which resembled the French landscape that inspired the Impressionists. They set up their canvases outdoors during all seasons, painting the picturesque scenes around them.

Influenced by the realism and illustration coming out of the Brandywine Valley, the New Hope School contributed its own imprint to American art, extending the era of Impressionism. Walter E. Baum (1884-1956), the only artist of this school who was a Bucks County native, painted regional landscapes and then founded the Baum School of Art and an art museum of Allentown; he plunged into German history, excelling as an art critic.

While the New Hope Group congregated at Phillips Mill near Lumberville, Chester County artists George Cope (1855-1929) and Ada Williamson (1880-1958) were reaching deep into their heritage for their art.

Many of these Pennsylvania Impressionists gained their realism at the Pennsylvania Academy of the Fine Arts in Philadelphia. In earlier years at the country's oldest art school, innovative Thomas Eakins (1844-1916) taught his students to draw the human figure from live models. His skill in presenting the structure of living things is evident in his works that hang at the Academy, an ornate building designed by Frank Furness (1839-1912), the City's master of Victorian Gothic-style buildings in the late 1800s. Eakins' dramatic use of light is evident in the work of students such as Henry O. Tanner (1859-1937). Some of Eakins' most popular works, for example, those of oarsmen on the Schuylkill, are in the American collection at the Philadelphia Museum of Art.

Visiting the city's acclaimed museum is a soul experience that begins upon approach. Its prime location indicates how much this city prizes art. Overlooking the Schuylkill, the Greek Revival edifice serves as the gateway of Fairmount Park and the finale of the Benjamin Franklin Parkway, a mile-long boulevard that resembles the Champs Élysées of Paris.

Since the museum was built in the 1920s, numerous outdoor sculptures have been added to its ten acres. They vary from equestrian statues to Revolutionary War heroes and fountains. One of the twin fountains on the Eakins Oval at the foot of the museum honors Eli Kirk Price II, a Philadelphia lawyer who waded through much criticism to construct the parkway and situate the museum on its present acropolis. To realize the boulevard that Price believed Fairmount Park deserved to bring its greenery to city center, many blocks of dwellings were flattened.

A few other sculptures give tribute to Philadelphians. Museum visitors who await the bus on the west terrace are in the presence of Stephen Girard, a merchant described in bronze as "Philadelphia's Greatest Philanthropist." His personal millions bailed out the national treasury during the War of 1812 and later, in 1846, established a school that is now Girard College.

The museum building itself *wears* sculpture in the form of thirteen striking polychrome terra-cotta statues across the tympanum of the North Wing. Up on the roof corners pose bronze griffins. Known to the Greeks as the guardians of treasure, they are symbols of the museum, which houses some 350,000 objects of art. More than 200 galleries feature Asian pieces that date back to 500 A.D. and Western art from the rise of Christendom. Among its decorative arts are Turkish carpets, Philadelphia silver and Chinese ceramics, as well as a Japanese tea house and a medieval stone abbey.

A $10 million reinstallation during the nineties integrated the renowned collection of John G. Johnson (1841-1917), creating a visual feast of 800 years of Western art from 1100 A.D. in "a cohesive, chronological manner." Johnson, an expert at corporate law, collected art with just as much finesse. He bequeathed his city's museum with one of the finest collections of Western art from the 14th to the 19th centuries. It includes such medieval treasures as Jan van Eyck's "Saint Francis Receiving the Stigmata," a miniature that becomes more meaningful when the guard lends a loupe to magnify the objects that were painted by three-bristle brushes. The brilliance that reaches deep into the scene's perspective stays with the viewer a long time.

The museum also administers the Rodin Museum which houses the largest collection of Auguste Rodin's (1840-1917) sculpture outside of Paris.

Philadelphia boasts another museum devoted to the works of a single artist. The Norman Rockwell Museum is located in the Curtis Building where the American illustrator dropped off the first of his covers at the editorial offices of the *Saturday Evening Post.* Today, Rockwell's (1894-1978) 324 *Post* covers and other paintings give viewers a bit of nostalgia that often brings a chuckle.

A wider scope of American visual arts, many from the Pennsylvania Impressionist and New Hope Schools, enrich the collections of the James A. Michener Art Museum in nearby historic Doylestown. This regional gem holds local, national and international material in superb light. Furnishings by world-renowned sculptor George Nakashima (1905-1990) grace a Reading Room that was designed by his daughter Mira Nakashima-Yarnall. The Japanese-style room reflects his respect for spirituality within nature and his practice of "listening" to the inherent qualities of unfinished wood. Some of the museum's state-of-the-art galleries offer a view of the Sculpture Garden whose backdrop is the old stone wall of an 1885 Gothic-style Bucks County prison that was designed by Addison Hutton of Philadelphia.

The museum remarkably encompasses the visual and literary arts. A permanent exhibit in the foyer ushers visitors into the Bucks County office where native James A. Michener (b. 1907) wrote *Tales of the South Pacific* among other major works. The display features the writer's commitment to racial harmony, to the humanities at their best and to satisfying his curiosity about the world. The exhibit also celebrates Michener as an art collector and philanthropist, roles that are most striking in a museum that bears his name in his hometown.

*Fraktur,* illuminated manuscripts, emerged as a folk art in German communities bounded by the Lehigh, Delaware and Schuylkill Rivers. Individuals drew colorful birds, flowers, symbols and sayings to decorate certificates or the flyleaf of a book. Christopher Dock (d. 1771), a Mennonite schoolmaster who taught at Germantown in the 1700s, drew *fraktur* for students deserving recognition; he stood out from cane-wielding teachers by encouraging his students with praise and kindness. *Fraktur,* with its tulips, finches and cedar trees, adorn birth certificates and songbooks given to people completing singing school. More than 120 pieces of *fraktur*, some by Dock, are in the collection of The Meetinghouse, a museum/historical library in Harleysville that presents Mennonite heritage and life. Its gift shop sells *fraktur* by several Mennonites, some of whom are schoolteachers.

In Philadelphia, rare book dealer A.S.W. Rosenbach and his brother, Philip, an authority on antiques, have left the public their exquisite townhouse and an unrivaled collection of the possessions of the royal rich and the literary famous. Traipsing to the Rosenbach Museum and Library at 2010 Delancey Place leads to one of the finest Victorian blocks in the city just two streets from Rittenhouse Square. In addition to fabulous furnishings, such as the chest where England's Charles II kept his papers, the museum's 30,000 books, 270,000 manuscript materials and 20,000 works of art on paper span from medieval Chaucer to Maurice Sendak, the 20th century children's book illustrator and author.

Among the literary treasures are James Joyce's handwritten manuscript of *Ulysses* and the finest first edition of Cervantes' *Don Quixote* . On exhibit is the furniture from the New York living room where poet Marianne Moore (1887-1972) wrote. The Rosenbachs left the best of the items that they garnered during a prime era for collecting, but the museum's holdings have grown 30 percent since it was founded in1954. This unique museum also shines as a research library for scholars.

In the 1990s, government and business boosted Center City's performing arts by investing $300 million to create galleries and performing arts spaces along the Avenue of the Arts. The bricks and mortar campaign created a vital district that encompasses 4.25 miles between Thompson and Lehigh Streets and City Hall to Washington Avenue.

A major component of the Avenue is a new concert hall designed to showcase the esteemed Philadelphia Orchestra. From its founding in 1900, the orchestra's home has been the Academy of Music, America's oldest grand opera house still used for its original purpose. Built in 1857, the opulent setting has been in great demand over the decades, serving the Pennsylvania Ballet, the Opera Company of Philadelphia, the All-Star Forum Great Performers Series, Peter Nero & the Philly Pops Concert Series and a host of other performing arts groups. Many of the century's great artists have performed at the Academy. The tenures of the Orchestra's notable musical directors—Leopold Stokowski, Eugene Ormandy, Riccardo Muti and, as of 1993, Wolfgang Sawallisch—add distinction to the Academy's history. The hall's plush interior appeared in the 1993 movie, *The Age of Innocence.*

There have always been plays in Philadelphia, even when they were banned by its Quaker founders. After the last ordinance against theatrical performances was repealed in 1789, a rash of performing arts venues rose across the city. Most went dark in time, and many have since disappeared. A building at 9th and Walnut that first housed a circus in 1809 remains. Walnut Street Theatre, the oldest theater in continuous use in the English-speaking world, has been on the cutting edge of stage drama since its first production in 1812. At this historic site, the first gas footlights and first air conditioning were installed in a theater. Here the custom of a curtain call began with the post-play appearance of Edmund Kean. Today this restored National Historic Landmark offers superb mainstage performances in a setting that was shared by many theater greats.

With Philadelphia the country's leading tourism destination for African-Americans, art centers featuring black culture are in demand. Several of the organizations receiving Avenue of the Arts funding serve African-American communities.

Drama lovers attend plays at the Freedom Theatre, one of the top six African-American theaters in the nation according to the JFK Center for Performing Arts. Presenting seven plays and training close to 800 students each year is an ambitious program that evolved since 1966. John E. Allen, Jr. (1934-92), one of the first black executives at Sun Oil, founded the theater because he enjoyed acting and saw a need for the depiction of African-American experience as a significant part of American society. Such stars as Pam Tyson, Lisa Summerour and Erika Alexander trained at Freedom, and many more people have gained self-esteem to launch them into successful careers outside of drama.

Besides being a strong neighborhood anchor, the theater's home has a rich history. As Heritage House, it was a vital hub for community organizing. Previously, it housed the first technical training institute for women, a precursor of Moore College of Art, and originally was the home of Edwin Forrest (1806-72), America's first internationally renowned tragic actor.

The Philadelphia Clef Club's home at the corner of Fitzwater and Broad Streets is the first American building that was constructed expressly for jazz. The Clef Club organized on the ashes of Local 274, a black musicians' union that lost its charter in 1971 after dual unionism was abolished. Such jazz greats as John Coltrane (1926-1963), Nina Simone (b. 1933) and "Dizzy" Gillespie (1917-1993) were among its members. The camaraderie that drew ethnic musicians together at the union's quarters for 36 years still sparks improvisation in the Clef Club's resident bands.

The arts abound in Philadelphia and the four counties that crescent it. Even as their various institutions wax and wane, people in the southeastern part of the state nurture an artistically fertile milieu. This is easily demonstrated in the contemporary works by 52 artists on permanent exhibit in the Philadelphia Convention Center. This display fulfills a City requirement that one percent of the cost of all public buildings be designated for art. This policy, and how it benefits the area, continues to make novelist Henry James' comment about Philadelphia ring true: "... of all goodly villages, the very goodliest, probably in the world; the very largest, ... and smoothest, the most rounded and complete." The arts of the region deserve the breadth of such superlatives.

*Following Pages* The neo-Baroque interior of the Academy of Music (1855-57) on S. Broad St. features a central chandelier.

*Left* Designed by Philadelphian Frank Furness (1839-1912), the Pennsylvania Academy of Fine Arts is one of the most magnificent Victorian buildings in the country. The Washington Foyer leads to the Museum's galleries. *Above* The pediment of the north wing of the Philadelphia Museum of Art exhibits bright terra-cotta figure sculptures.

*Above* The Great Stair Hall is an imposing interior feature of the Philadelphia Museum of Art. *Top Right* Works by Thomas Eakins (1844-1916) are a part of the museum's American Collection. *Bottom* One of the museum's period rooms is the drawing room from the Lansdowne House in London, which was designed by Robert Adam (1728-92).

*Left* *The Thinker* and *The Gates of Hell*, sculptures by Auguste Rodin (1840-1917) grace the entrance to the Rodin Museum on the Ben Franklin Parkway. *Center* In Bucks County's James A. Michener Art Museum the Changing Exhibitions Gallery balances indirect natural and artificial light. *Right* Under a conservancy, The Brandywine River Museum in Chester County upholds the integration of art, environment and history.

*Above Left* Designed by Mira Nakashima-Yarnall as a memorial to her sculptor father George Nakashima (1905-90), the Reading Room at James A. Michener Museum is Japanese in style. *Above Right* Wharton Esherick (1887-1970), a wood sculptor, left his Chester County home and studio. Its architecture and furnishings reveal his imaginative skills over a 50-year span. *Top Right* Author Pearl Buck wrote *The Good Earth* at the desk in the library of her Bucks County home. *Bottom* The Brandywine River Museum near Chadds Ford exhibits works of the Wyeth family.

# GARDENS AND ARBORETUMS

*Southeastern Pennsylvania is America's horticultural heaven. Here, interest in plants is so* widespread that more than 5,000 locals turn out for a plant fair at an arboretum. The floral and fountain displays at Longwood Gardens, the polestar of North American gardens, attract at least 800,000 annual visitors from around the globe. Each March, Philadelphia hosts the largest indoor flower show in the world. Within the scenic valleys of the Schuylkill and Delaware Rivers, parks and conservancies showcase and safeguard natural beauty. And many residents tuck a new hybrid into their already abundant gardens.

Philadelphia and its countryside holds a legacy of greenery that trails back to the Native Americans who traversed Pennsylvania for 10,000 years before the Europeans arrived. The Delaware Valley was home to the Unami, one of three divisions of the Lenni-Lenape or Delawares. Of these "people of the forest," William Penn wrote almost poetically, "...their pleasure feeds them,... their Hunting, Fishing and Fowling, and this Table is spread every where; the Woods and Rivers are their Larder."

The Delawares gleaned no more than they needed from land that they declined to own and agreed to share. By 1700, these original Americans had slipped in numbers and in power, marking their environment lightly. The next settlers, however, laid out roads and constructed barns and large dwellings from their European experience.

Many early colonists were Quakers and brought with them the belief that an apprecia-

*"Those seeds that in England take fourteen days to rise, are up here in six or seven days. ...we have excellent Trees, Shrubs, and Flowers & Herbs here, which I did not know I ever saw in any Gardens in England."*

*William Penn*

tive understanding of nature would help them know God's ways.

Their English founder, George Fox, promoted teaching gardening, even suggesting during a visit to America in 1690 that some of the land that he bequeathed to Philadelphia Quakers be cultivated with "Physical Plants, for Lads and Lasses to know Simples...."

With support of gardening strong in Quakerism, it is not totally surprising that in 1798, twin brothers of that faith, Samuel and Joshua Peirce, began planting rows of ornamental trees on the Kennett Square farm that had been a Penn grant to their great-grandfather. Out of their knapsacks came seedlings, including such rare ones as the yellow-flowered cucumber magnolia from Georgia. The Peirces kept collecting, and over the next 50 years, the trees matured into one of the finest arboretums in the country. In the late 1800s, at the invitation of Joshua's son George, people gathered for recreation—boating, picnicking and croquet—in Peirce's Park.

Public visitation continues today since 1906, when Pierre Samuel du Pont bought the deteriorating park to save its trees from the sawmill that had been set up on the property. A chemist who had inherited a fondness for plants from his great-grandfather, du Pont was attracted to the beautiful old trees that he had fortuitously saved on a whim during an outing. The purchase, which du Pont called an "attack of insanity," plunged this corporate genius into his life-long avocation of gardening. With extensive knowledge, care and money, he nurtured the 202 acres into the world-famous Longwood Gardens.

Visitors exclaim over the artful flower displays indoors and throughout the grounds that now total 1,050 acres. This horticultural spectacle blooms even in January and is open every day of the year. Conservatory blossoms planted around lush green grass vary with the seasons. Cyclamens and tulips look brilliant against the snow outside the high arched windows. Each fall, the famous Chrysanthemum Festival features 15,000 mums in cascades, pillars and hanging globes.

During summer, there is exquisite beauty in the five waterlily pools. Most intriguing are the rimmed hybrid waterplatters with leaves that reach up to seven feet in diameter. They grow from pea-size seeds that are bred by crossing two parent species.

On a grand scale, colored lights, fountains, fireworks and music combine to dazzle summer visitors. Such entertainment ideas came from du Pont, who expanded Longwood as his corporations flourished. A stroll under the large trees in Peirce's Park, or to gardens such as the Waterfall or Italian Water Garden, is a reminder that much original planning has gone into creating Longwood's beauty over the past 200 years.

This showplace is also a research and training axis. Here new varieties, such as the New Guinea impatiens and aquatic canna, were developed and released to homeowners. Through the continuing education courses, gardeners and nurserymen gain knowledge that perpetually upgrades the public's "green thumb."

Area colleges such as Haverford, Bryn Mawr and Swarthmore, all Quaker originals, join Longwood Gardens in propelling horticulture to new levels of sophistication. At Haverford in Delaware County, a pinetum that was planted in 1928 features 332 conifers arranged according to genus and family. On Bryn Mawr's campus, many century-old trees add grandeur to the stone Collegiate Gothic-style buildings.

Scott Arboretum's headquarters near Swarthmore's main entrance indicates its prime role. By distributing free houseplants to students and identifying every plant on campus, the College underlines their value for students and the community. The Arboretum's 300 acres display more than 5,000 kinds of ornamental plants. The textures and colors of foliage and blossoms harmonize in the Teaching Garden.

Along the Mainline, Villanova University's campus is dedicated as a public arboretum. A self-guiding walk goes past magnificent beeches and redwoods.

In the fertile milieu of southeastern Pennsylvania, garden gurus are realizing their horticultural visions. Earl Jamison, who gained appreciation for the soft and flowing qualities of nature as a boy on a Bucks County farm, designed the award-winning landscaping at Peddler's Village in Lahaska.

The varied shapes of shrubs and conifers blend as sculptures adorning the shops and restaurants. Jamison feels that "there is much beauty in variations of green."

The greens of 30 indigenous mosses are the high point of David E. Benner's shade garden near New Hope. In 1962, this Bucks County environmentalist "began to work with nature" on two acres that now feature wildflowers, ferns, moss lawns and deciduous trees.

A much more formal garden, Chanticleer, uses its open spaces to feature floriculture. This pleasure garden in Wayne reflects careful blending of plants and land contours. Landscaping ideas abound at this 30-acre estate of the Adolf Rosengarten family. The visual show of flowering trees, masses of daffodils and many species of meadow blooms draw visitors from April through the end of October.

Morris and Tyler Arboretums were both developed on estates, the former by John T. Morris and his sister Lydia on their 166 acres in Chestnut Hill, and the latter by two Quaker brothers, Minshall and Jacob Painter on 700 acres of their family farm near Media in Delaware County.

Tyler's spring show is a hillside of mountain phlox and collections of rhododendrons and azaleas. In addition to many of the thousand trees that the Painters put in between 1830 and 1875, plantings of holly trees, flowering ornamentals and conifers draw visitors year-round.

A stroll through the Morris Arboretum is an invitation to learn about 6,700 plants and shrubs from around the world, all identified. Between April and October, visitors can enjoy the oak allée, an azalea meadow, a terrace rose garden and a swan pond, as well as mature and thriving trees. An interdisciplinary center of the University of Pennsylvania, the arboretum also maintains a database of the flora of Pennsylvania. The project includes monitoring the state's 349 native plants that are on lists of rare, threatened and endangered species.

Bartram's Garden, the oldest garden devoted to the native plants of America, is in West Philadelphia near a trolley route. How remarkable that this 45-acre botanical garden, the country's oldest, still survives in an industrial landscape.

Today from the wildflower meadow of Historic Bartram's Garden, the geometric shapes of the downtown skyline rise above rich-petaled daisies. In the 1730s, John Bartram (1699-1777), a Quaker farmer, was ploughing at this same site when he stopped and noticed a daisy.

Close observation moved him to devote his life to

studying nature. He started by borrowing books. With Latin tutoring on top of his fourth-grade education, Bartram quickly learned to read the writings of Linneaus, the father of binary nomenclature in science.

As the royal botanist from 1765 until the revolution broke out, Bartram sent King George III samples of New World plants. Via letters sent with seed shipments to an English buyer Peter Collinson, it is known that Bartram introduced more than 200 new American native plants to European gardens.

A masterful observer of nature, Bartram cultivated the famous Franklin tree, a tree with striking white blooms from Georgia, that he named after his longtime friend Benjamin Franklin. Bartram concocted rhubarb pie after Franklin sent him the plant from England.

Bartram's son ,William (1739-1823), joined his father on collecting trips way into the frontier. Well-educated, he thrived on the natural sciences, eventually writing and sketching the flora and fauna that he found during his own four-year journey through southern habitats. Titled *Travels,* this scientifically detailed journal has been cited by many poets and botanists. Later in 1783, Bartram's Garden published the first plant catalog in the United States.

At Historic Bartram's Garden today grow many of the tree species that were collected by father and son between 1728 and 1823. A ramble past the fine masonry of the stone buildings leads to towering gingko trees and such natives as pawpaw and tulip trees to bald cypress at the river's edge.

Other historic gardens delight visitors. In Germantown, the garden at Wyck grows with parterres according to its original early nineteenth century plan. A June feature is the blooms of 38 varieties of old roses. Nearby, the Ebenezer Maxwell Mansion boasts a noteworthy Victorian garden.

Horticulture has always been valued in Philadelphia. What began with founder William Penn's vision of a "Greene Countrie Towne" laid out between the watery corridors of two rivers, is now a city with a quarter-million trees and more than 8,800 acres in parkland. Under Penn's direction, Surveyor-General Thomas Holme set aside a square for recreation within each of the Great Towne's four quadrants.

Three centuries later, there is grassy shade, benches and gravel pathways at these squares—Franklin, Washington, Rittenhouse—and Logan Circle. This last one boasts the invigorating sound of water flowing around three reclining nudes who represent Philadelphia's three rivers, figures sculpted by Alexander Stirling Calder (1898-1976). On hot days, children splash in the basin of the fountain, and parades skirt it, flowing in the direction of Fairmount Park, the largest municipal park in the country. With trails, historic homes, statues and sports facilities, the park system spreads along both banks of the Schuylkill River but also includes land along smaller waterways and pocket parks.

The northernmost point of Fairmount Park offers such esoteric seclusion that it can be aptly called "an inner city wilderness." The trail along Wissahickon Creek—no motor vehicles, please —winds through a gorge of mature heaths, hemlocks and cascades. Deer, waterfowl and songbirds live in this wild haven that has been a retreat for generations of city residents. People jog, pedal and stroll, inhaling the creek's beauty as it flows south, dropping 100 feet in 6.5 miles. When Fairmount Park swooped up the Wissahickon gorge in 1868, it brought an end to all the manufacturing that had been built on this creek's waterpower over the previous century. Nature at its pristine best took over and has been in charge since, with help from Friends of the Wissahickon.

Long-time commitment to horticulture has harvested appreciation for green growth throughout the Delaware Valley. In Philadelphia, the Pennsylvania Horticultural Society operates the nation's largest urban greening program. Since 1974, Philadelphia Green has helped neighborhoods plant and design food and flower gardens and landscape inhospitable public areas. Thousands of volunteers have planted bright, verdant patches and have beautified unsightly urban routes. In the nineties, the society and corporate partners rehabilitated the four-acre Azalea Garden behind the art museum. Many newlyweds pose for photos each spring among the neon-bright heaths.

Funds for greening projects originate from the society's annual flower show, the oldest and most prestigious in the nation. Started in 1829, the show has been a venue for introducing new plant material; in fact, the pointsettia debuted here. Each March, displays by talented gardeners from around the world fill six acres of indoor exhibit space. The show's thousands of plants and flowers, forced into bloom indoors, delight visitors for a week. During the show, the city becomes a "Green Countrie Towne" even in winter.

The event verifies that Philadelphia and its countryside is the crown jewel of American horticulture.

*Above* Each March in Philadelphia, the Horticultural Society presents the largest indoor flower show in the world. *Following Pages* Longwood Gardens' Chrysanthemum Festival features mums in cascades, pillars, hanging globes as well as in a garden grouping like these spider mums.

*Top Left* The Peirce-du Pont house was the farm-house of the two Quaker brothers who nurtured an arboretum, which was the horticultural foundation of today's Longwood Gardens. *Bottom Left* Poin-settias glamorize the holiday show. *Bottom Right* Orchids are in bloom for visitors every day of the year. *Center* Waterlily ponds attract Amish visitors in summer. *Right* Fireworks and a lighted fountain show enhance the summer beauty of the outdoor gardens and conservatories at Longwood.

*Top Left* The gardens of Longview Farm have been
included on Chester County Day, an annual tour of
lovely properties. *Bottom Left* Horticultural landscaping draws crowds to the Philadelphia Flower Show.
*Bottom Right* Bulbs spring into bloom at Chas.
H. Mueller Co., north of New Hope. *Above* Peddler's
Village, Lahaska, features Earl Jamison's landscaping.

 *Above* The Scott Arboretum at Swarthmore College features ornamentals. *Top Right* A garden enhances the 18th century stone homes along Court Street in Newtown, Bucks County. *Bottom* Patio plantings lure visitors to walk around Chanticleer, a pleasure garden on a 30-acre estate near Wayne.

# REPAST & RESPITE AT HISTORIC INNS

*Taverns and inns were the main inland transportation stops of 18th century* Pennsylvania. In Bucks County, 54 public lodging houses kept travellers fed and rested at the time of the Revolutionary War. Today, staying at a site that made history is intriguing, and the cuisine far exceeds the simple but filling fare of the past. For instance, guests at Chef Tell's Harrow Inn in the town of Ottsville relish *schweinepfeffer,* a pork dish with peppers and mushrooms, a speciality compared to the staples served when it was a stagecoach stop in the years following its 1744 opening.

Farther east along River Road stands the Isaac Stover House, a Victorian Federal mansion that was built by a German settler c. 1837; ornate touches were added by a later owner. Sitting on the porch facing the Delaware provides a majestic moment.

Along the same route, from Lumberville's Black Bass Hotel, an open dining room overlooks the river and a walking bridge across it. Canal workers of the 1800s—and early 20th century artists such as Edward W. Redfield (1865-1965), Fern Coppedge (1883-1968) and Robert Spencer (1879-1931) who put this neighborhood on canvas—all must have enjoyed this venue. The hotel displays a large collection of British royal memorabilia, including paintings of Queen Victoria and such esoteric objects as a leaf from Sherwood Forest.

A night at Ash Mill Farm, a 1790 manor, can only be surpassed by returning for another in a different season. Whether fireflies light up at dusk or flecks of starlight dazzle a cold sky,

*"I thank God I came...; find the land good,...beef, mutton, veal, pork, all sorts of admirable foul, good venison, bread, butter, beer and cider not inferior to England...."*

*—William Penn*

there is an earthy scent and a country welcome at this bed and breakfast along the old York Road. Sheep mill about in the meadow year-round.

The spacious fireside parlour at the Barley Sheaf Farm brings to mind the dramatic whirl that this 1780s stone house witnessed when playwright George Kaufman lived here for 17 years in the 1930s, entertaining the likes of Dorothy Parker and Harpo Marx. Rambling about the 30 acres reveals typical Bucks County images: a rowboat mirrored in a small pond, reeds near a footbridge and a stream that gurgles as it must have when the last Lenni-Lenape encampment was made on this land.

The Inn at Fordhook Farm is a 60-acre estate that was once the home of W. Atlee Burpee, founder of the Burpee Seed Company. Here growing things comes naturally and guests enjoy scenic gardens, meadows and woodlands as well as family antiques throughout the whole house.

Another site for guests to relive recent history is Highland Farms, the home of lyricist, Oscar Hammerstein, who wrote "Oklahoma," "Carousel" and "Sound of Music" here. Each of the bedrooms at this Doylestown bed and breakfast are named for one of his famed musicals.

With a Halloween howl rattling the windows, the warm comforter on the bed in Carrie's Loft made the night at Ye Old Temperance House in Newtown snuggly warm. This inn's 13 rooms, each with its own name and mood, and eight dining areas still feed and bed guests as they did in 1772. The walk-in fireplace discovered behind a wall in the dining room during a recent restoration is a real gem. The fieldstone hearth had two bread ovens intact and a copper kettle hanging in place. Today diners in four rooms enjoy a roaring fire as they feast on the chef's specialties.

Houses of lodging rose at crossroads and busy routes throughout the 18th century. The Sign of the Sorrel Horse is a 1749 stone inn near Quakertown. Its low ceilings and the scent of wood smoke create an ambience of the past that enhances the distinctive, contemporary menu items. The restored Historic General Warren Inne is located one block from Route 30 on Old Lancaster Highway and offers dining and lodging as it did in 1745. Along Skippack Pike, a route that the patriot troops travelled, today's Blue Bell Inn gave General George Washington lodging in 1777. It was then called the White Horse Inn.

Sweetwater Farm Bed and Breakfast, a 1734 Georgian mansion with a five-story bank barn, beds guests in hand-stenciled rooms. Pace One Restaurant and Country Inn is a 250-year-old fieldstone barn that has been converted into an exquisite restaurant. Surviving the Battle of Brandywine, it is the gathering point in the little Chester County hamlet of Thornton.

Today, as guests dine on the porch of the Inn at Yellow Springs, they enjoy a scenic view of Yellow Springs, a settlement that also had a Continental Army Hospital 1777-1781. In peaceful times before and after the Revolution, people sought overnight lodging in this town near Chester Springs to benefit from its several active mineral springs. Such colonial notables as George Washington and James Monroe are believed to have visited this health spa, taking advantage of the iron spring whose yellow waters gave Yellow Springs its name.

To relive our country's independence experience begs for a meal at the reconstructed City Tavern in Philadelphia. Built in 1773, the original was frequented by our nation-builders. The wood plank floors and small-paned windows of today's rebuilt inn, within the jurisdiction of Independence National Historical Park, suggests 18th century basics. It is easy to imagine debate-weary delegates becoming animated over ale and lamb in such a setting. Members of the Continental Congresses and the Constitutional Convention frequented its bar and dining rooms, reminding present diners that camaraderie figured in on the building of our national government. A leader whose words were never effusive, John Adams, called it "the most genteel tavern" in America.

A block away but still in the park is the historic home of the Philadelphia physician and surgeon, Thomas Bond, now an elegant bed and breakfast with 12 guest rooms. Decorated with Federal-style furnishings, the 18th century rooms offer 20th century comforts. Relaxing in front of the Rumford fireplace in the parlour or eating a hearty breakfast in the dining room invites guests to slow their pace.

Bond built this four-story Georgian house in 1769, some years after he helped his friends Benjamin Franklin and Benjamin Rush found the Pennsylvania Hospital, the city's first public hospital. The creak of a carriage outside on South Second Street is a reminder that many of Bond's contemporaries were also doers—astronomer David Rittenhouse and Robert Fulton, who experimented with steam power. In 1699, William Penn had rented the Slate Roof House from a friend; its site across the street is now Welcome Park, which features the proprietor's views and achievements.

During that same visit to Pennsylvania, Penn and his daughter Letitia spent a night at the home of a Welsh Quaker Thomas Evans enroute from Philadelphia. Today that dwelling (after much expansion) is known as the William Penn Inn at Gwynedd, serving a well-seasoned snapper soup as one of the favorites of its continental American cuisine. There are four top-floor suites beside numerous dining rooms.

Stone and brick colonial dwellings where history was made nestle in the idyllic countryside and offer respite and repast to anyone who is renewed by the call of the mourning dove and the rush of a rock-strewn creek below a covered bridge. Nowhere in America are 18th century country inns and B&Bs so plentiful or the winding roads to them as scenic.

*Top Left* With its unusual twig furniture, The Benetz Suite is as distinctive as the other rooms at The Temperance House (c. 1772), Newtown. *Bottom* A mural in a dining room of The Temperance House, Newtown, portrays the "peaceable kingdom" theme used by the Quaker artist Edward Hicks (d. 1849) who lived in this Bucks County town. *Above* "The Conservatory" is an indoor garden cafe at Hotel Atop the Bellevue, Philadelphia's historic hotel of French Renaissance style. As installed by hotelier George Boldt in the Bellevue-Stratford (1904), today's restored hotel retains the Thomas Edison light fixtures and ballroom where the city's elite gather for the Assembly Ball.

*Previous Pages* The spacious porch at Ash Mill Farm, Holicong, invites one to enjoy the bucolic outdoors that has attracted artists and travellers to Bucks County since the 18th century. *Top Left* Hotel du Village, a country inn on 10 acres near New Hope, is situated on a Penn grant. *Bottom Left* The parlour of the Barley Sheaf Bed and Breakfast in Bucks County once reverberated with the voices of the guests of playwright George Kaufman. *Bottom Right* A Federalist mansion, Hamanassett is a B&B in quiet Lima, Chester Co. *Above* In 1745 guests dined at the Historic General Warren Inne, Malvern.

98

*Top Left* Now offering hearthside dining, the Dilworthtown Inn near West Chester provided food and lodging to travellers back in 1754. *Bottom* The Logan, a restored 1727 inn and restaurant, was the first place of lodging in New Hope, now a quaint riverside village of shops and galleries in Bucks County. *Above* Guests enjoy antiques and treasures from numerous countries at the Isaac Stover House along the Delaware River.

# COUNTY SEATS AND HAMLETS

*In the beginning, there were no towns in Pennsylvania, only forests. But tradition recalls* that while William Penn was riding horseback along a trail in the woods, no doubt pondering on the value of settlement within his colony, he paused at the present site of Newtown in Bucks County and declared, "This is the place proposed for my new town." The name stuck as Penn demonstrated his desire that towns be planned as well as his City of Brotherly Love. To entice buyers, the proprietor offered town plots equivalent to 10 percent of the size of a township lot purchased plus common grazing lands. By 1716, 40 acres on both sides of Newtown Creek and its springs were owned commonly for water and pasture. Today, most of that land is in private hands. A mere marker on a grassy patch near the creek is shared by Newtown's 2,500 plus residents.

With two-thirds of this historic borough part of a National Historic District, heritage threads daily existence here. Along State Street continental flags with 13 stars in a circle whip in the breeze above benches with decorative ironwork. Charming shops stock cards, books, stationery and some untraditional products such as pizza to bake at home.

Locals are lined up at the counter of the Newtown Hardware House, a store with bins and wooden cases that look as though they have been there since its opening in 1869.

Across the street is a restored frame house, built before 1690 which was once the Bird in Hand tavern. Its sign—and many others painted in the town in the 1820s—were made

*"Governments, like clocks, go from the motion men give them...."*

*William Penn*

by Edward Hicks, a Quaker primitive artist who is better known for his Peaceable Kingdom paintings. He lived at 122 Penn Street until his death in 1849; his gravesite rests in the shaded cemetery of the Friends Meetinghouse on Court Street.

The small fieldstone houses on this block create a quaint sense of times past, when the residents were making carriages and leather boots. An 18th century tavern is located within the Court Inn, headquarters of the Newtown Historic Association.

A stretch of Delaware River falls that required disembarking became a reason for a 17th century settlement, Fallsington. Its location was an appropriate stop along the King's Highway, the main colonial route north to New York. Today's Route 13 was once a Native American path to jasper mines.

Fallsington's first building, a 1690 Quaker meetinghouse, no longer exists, but three meetinghouses on the town square where five roads meet proclaim a long-term tie to the Religious Society of Friends. Founder William Penn worshipped here, travelling by horse and wagon from Pennsbury, his country manor along the Delaware River. The oldest standing meetinghouse dates back to 1729; a larger 1789 house of worship is used as a daycare while the 1841 stone meetinghouse serves an active group of Quakers. All of the buildings on the square were built no later than the 1840s.

It was the threat of the bulldozing of the Burgess-Lippincott House on the Square that galvanized area folks in 1953 to form Historic Fallsington, Inc., a non-profit organization to preserve this prerevolutionary village as a heritage museum. It interprets six buildings and the town, a historic oasis in the midst of rampant industry and full-scale suburbia. Visitors can observe varied architectural motifs, such as the tooling on the Federal door of the Burgess-Lippincott House.

Beside the Delaware River in upper Bucks, New Hope packs an artful wallop. In the summer, crowds give Main Street a beachside mood. Anyone for plum brandy ice cream? Colorful shops, galleries and restaurants shoulder each other.

Within a few short blocks, transportation modes from the past slow the pulse of activities. The river, typically serene, sports rides on Coryell's Ferry to relax. (Yes, General Washington tried it, too.) Life goes even more slowly floating on the Delaware Canal at 4 mph. Along the canal towpath, a jogger passes the mules pulling the barge. Moths flit above the water. Flowers in window boxes catch the afternoon sun. The tables at a waterside cafe are crowded. The barge glides under a hump-backed bridge and past several aqueducts. This must be Pennsylvania's Venice.

It's time to catch the train to Lahaska from the station at Bridge and Stockton Streets. The New Hope and Ivyland Railroad offers steam passenger service with narration on the 50-minute ride and perhaps some music on the platform.

A summer day in New Hope often ends with a play at the Bucks County Playhouse in a former grist mill that was built by a settler as promised to William Penn. Even when he was handing out large grants, Penn was focused on land development for economic gain.

Bucks County's seat, Doylestown, has two castles, both built by Henry Chapman Mercer (1856-1930), architect, collector and ceramist. The structure of one, the Mercer Museum, fits its contents, tools of the preindustrial age. The Central Court exhibits pieces as large as a whaleboat and a gristmill, while around it, early American artifacts are displayed on six levels with ceilings of varying heights. A walk-through is a most unconventional museum experience that stirs curiosity about his other castle and home, Fonthill.

Also built of concrete, the sprawling structure —yes, there are 44 rooms and 18 fireplaces—demonstrates vision and improvisation. Mercer's passions for historical research, archaeology and tile-making are evident in this medieval-type manor that was blessed with modern conveniences. While living on family money, Mercer also set up a pottery to follow his constant "longing to open a new door." Today, the Moravian Pottery and Tile Works reproduces and sells Mercer's original line of tiles, using his methods. Part of his legacy is a bird sanctuary and an arboretum of native trees marked with Mercer tiles behind Fonthill.

From his home, Mercer frequently biked to the museum while it was under construction, often passing but never greeting a small boy who lived across the street. Today, that lad now grown, James A. Michener, also has a museum named after him in Doylestown. After giving the world a bookshelf of superb novels and books on art, this writer and collector placed his financial and artistic support behind the Michener Art Museum, a repository for the visual arts of Bucks County. Locals worked enthusiastically to turn the town's abandoned prison into a regional polestar for art.

Near a bend of the Schuylkill lies Norristown, a borough of 35,000 that became the seat of Montgomery County in 1784 when there were fewer than 800 residents. Canals and textile mills attracted immigrants, and they stayed. At a recent community meeting when a millionaire businessman introduced himself, he never mentioned his firm. Instead, he noted, "I was born and raised here and graduated from Norristown High in 1927." Residents are proud of their local allegiance.

"Norristonians" also left their homes unchanged. In the early eighties, two large historic districts made the national registry. The Central Historic District encompasses 1,800 structures within approximately 40 blocks, most built before 1910. There are many storefronts, although the downtown lost its department stores when the King of Prussia Mall, the largest enclosed one in the East, opened its first segment near the turnpike in the sixties.

Many of the 1,700 homes in the West End Historic District feature fine brickwork and wrought iron made by Italian immigrants. Along Haws Avenue, an architectural feast, is a two-block stretch with five churches.

Further upriver stands Pottstown, a borough of more than 21,000, that grew up on the economic bedrock of iron and steel. In 1752, ironmaster John Potts laid out the town, the first in Montgomery County, and built a substantial home for his growing family on a site overlooking his own Pottsgrove Furnace.

When his mansion was completed after two years, people rode horseback as far as 30 miles to ooh and aah over its features—fieldstone walls two feet thick; windows even on the fourth floor and fine cornices. Today, visitors tour Pottsgrove Manor and see the exquisite woodworking on the mantles and corner cupboards; they learn of a first-rate manager who gained wealth from forges and furnaces and respect from his community for his integrity.

Along Route 73 between Gratersford Prison and Evansburg Park, both state-run, is Skippack Village, a mecca of country stores that have been drawing people since they came by trolley at the turn of the century.

West Chester has the most scenic approach of any borough in southeastern Pennsylvania. Tall sycamores grandly line both sides of Route 100, their boughs forming a welcoming canopy to High Street and the heart of the downtown. There are enough 19th century Greek Revival structures along the main street to call West Chester the "Athens of Pennsylvania." A splendid example is the courthouse, designed by Thomas U. Walter (1804-87), who apprenticed here before moving on to such projects as the U.S. Capitol dome.

Several buildings, including one on the campus of West Chester University (which almost doubles this town's population), were built with green serpentine stone mined from local quarries that are now closed.

West Chester is the seat of Pennsylvania's first county, Chester. At the museum of the historical society are artifacts that demonstrate the skills of the area's early settlers—fine clocks, intricate ironware and the free-flowing "line and berry" inlay on furniture. On display is the sign for the Turk's Head Tavern, which was located at a crossroads that stimulated the town's development.

A sense of the past remains beyond the museum. Charming Victorian-style homesteads surrounded with beds of ivy and flowers blend heritage and habitat. Many of the roads that trickle out of town lead to rolling horse country and substantial barns, a long rural tradition. In 1683, the Assembly chose a plough to be on the seal of Chester County.

The location of Chester was first considered for Penn's city, but its harbor was too shallow. A 1774 visitor wrote that Chester's neat brick buildings reminded him of Chelsea near London. It quickly became an industrial center with Penn investing in a grain mill. Today its old court house strikes a historical chord, but most of its streets are small-town 20th century America. With similar characteristics, Media is the crossroads seat of Delaware County.

The Main Line is a string of villages; several of them owe their existence to the railroad. The Paoli Local, a commuter train that has traversed approximately 20 miles from downtown Philly to Parkesburg since 1832, still links the city to the country homes of many of the executives and professionals it needs during the work week.

Many of the original residents moved from the city because they were lured by rail company slogans to "the locality where refinement resides and comfort creates its home." The next segment of the campaign pushed year-round residency so that that became the norm with the Poconos and New Jersey beaches evolving into a summer destination. Developers adopted names such as Narberth, Wynnewood and Berwyn to retain the Welsh heritage of the original settlers.

Established at the end of the 19th century, Bryn Mawr, Wayne and then Devon were planned residential communities with large lots, handsomely landscaped with ornamental shrubs. Buyers of plots in Wayne, for example, could select a home design from about 10 different styles. Residential hideaways grew up behind Route 30 and the railroad, parallel thoroughfares. With sidewalks leading to its shops, the Wayne Hotel gathering visitors and locals, and civic organizations connecting residents, Wayne upholds the flavor of a New England village.

Because they have more buildings than houses, towns, boroughs and hamlets are a compelling and intriguing entity. Penn felt that they deserved some planning. Even though malls attract many suburban shoppers, going to town still has an aura of excitement when you can explore such places as West Chester, Doylestown, New Hope and Newtown.

*Right* Architect Thomas U. Walter (1804-87) designed the courthouse in West Chester, the seat of Chester County.

*Above* The homes along New Street in West Chester, a borough of 18,000, blend heritage and beauty. *Top Right* Villanova University is along the Main Line, a string of boroughs and spacious residential areas on both sides of Route 30 and the railroad. *Bottom Left* Among other locally made pieces, on exhibit at the Chester County Historical Society are two portraits by Benjamin West made in his early teens and a walnut desk-on-frame, 1710-1740. *Bottom Right* As governor of Pennsylvania, Samuel W. Pennypacker (1843-1916) established the state police, which contributed to the safety of towns. His portrait (1897) by J.B. Sword hangs at Pennypacker Mills, his mansion home in Schwenksville, Montgomery County.

*Above* Doylestown, the county seat of Bucks, has known the influence of Henry Mercer (1856-1930), ceramist and collector. The walls of his concrete manor, Fonthill, are decorated with hand-painted tiles of Mercer's design. *Top Right* With 55 exhibit rooms and alcoves, the Mercer Museum, also in Doylestown, displays "the objects used by 18th and 19th century Americans to meet their everyday needs and wants." *Bottom Left* An artisan at The Moravian Tileworks paints one of the mosaic tiles, made Mercer-style at the pottery. *Bottom Right* Many 19th century Doylestown homes have interesting architectural details. The Dr. James Rich House (c.1824) on E. State St. intermingles Federal and Georgian features.

ST OFFICE

BOOKSTOR

Bicycle Rentals

LUMBERVILLE
STORE

1770

*Previous Pages* Lumberville Post Office lives out Americans' nostalgic image of the village gathering point. It is in the heart of Lumberville, a hamlet along Route 32 beside the Delaware in upper Bucks County. *Top Left* Signs and greenery distinguish town sites, here in Newtown, Bucks County. *Bottom Left* An inviting porch and homestead in Historic Yellow Springs, a community with mineral springs that attracted people during the 18th and 19th centuries. *Above* Located at a crossroads, the Brick Hotel in Newtown has served travellers since stagecoach days.

*Top Left* In New Hope the 1784 Parry Mansion is a house museum that was built by a mill owner. *Center* The charm of New Hope comes from its quaint shops, imaginative facades and narrow alleyways that lead to picturesque views of the canal and river. *Bottom* Carriage rides in New Hope can lead to getaways such as the Wedgwood Inn, a Victorian B & B on W. Bridge St. *Above* A medicine show from a bygone era entertains passengers waiting at the station of the New Hope & Ivyland RailRoad, a steam train service that began in 1891.

*Previous Pages* The parlor at Pennypacker Mills near Schwenksville reflects Governor Samuel W. Pennypacker's penchant for collecting. *Top Left* Mennonite communities benefited from the inspiration of *fraktur,* illustrated manuscripts, here on exhibit at The Meetinghouse, a Mennonite museum in Harleysville. *Center* Pottsgrove Manor was the home of John Potts, a colonial ironmaster who founded the borough of Pottstown in Montgomery County. *Bottom* This fanlight is an architectural detail at Graeme Park, a 1720s Horsham mansion that is the only remaining residence of a colonial Pennsylvania governor. *Above* Erwin-Stover House (1800) is the restored home of John Stover, who managed a farm and two mills. It is located in the first of Bucks County's parks.

*Top Left* The campus of Swarthmore College, one of several in Pennsylvania's southeast that were founded by Quakers, is an arboretum. *Top Right* The All-American Band from West Chester performs at Rose Tree Park, Media; this is one of numerous outdoor free concerts here each summer. *Bottom* Hope Lodge is a house museum in Montgomery County that reflects the design of its original mid-18th century owner, Quaker businessman Samuel Morris and the Colonial Revival decorations of Alice and William Degn, 20th century residents who were antique collectors. *Above* A county seat along the Schuylkill, Norristown has two large historic districts.

# THE WAYS OF THE COUNTRYSIDE

*Along a narrow winding road in upper Bucks County lies a picturebook farm scene. Their* bells tinkling, sheep graze in a lush meadow near a shed with a mossy, wood-shingled roof. Geese skim across a little pond while ducks preen near a paddlewheel that turns with water power. A rooster and guineas cross the road at will. Chickens scratch on the ground outside a little frame house. On the wooden porch are the memorabilia of country life—a cat curled on the rocking chair, a potted geranium. It all evokes a sense of nostalgia.

Parents often stop so their preschoolers can observe and even feed the animals that help to create this idyllic scene. And that's what it is, a symbol of what farm life was. This property is registered as a set, not a working farm. It fills a vital role in a county where farms have decreased but love of the life has not.

As the population soars across Pennsylvania's southeast, "entertainment farms" are replacing the traditional raising of grains and livestock. Farms and orchards sell a good time by advertising an event where people can pet animals, ride hay wagons, hear music and play old-fashioned games. At Nonesuch Farm in Bucks County, school groups and weekend visitors pay to pick a fall pumpkin from the field and learn about the squash family. This 400-acre farm has diversified by putting on a festival as well as selling fresh vegetables in season.

Direct marketing became a natural for farmers when housing developments started sprouting up around their fields. In the counties bordering Philly—Bucks, Montgomery,

*"The country life is to be preferred, for there we see the works of God; but in cities, little else but the works of men: and the one makes a better subject for our contemplation than the other."*

*William Penn*

Chester and Delaware—orchards offer just-picked fruit or pick-your-own. Strawberries turn ripe-red in May, and from then on the growing season produces cherries, blueberries, raspberries, peaches, pears and plums. More than a hundred varieties of apples grow in this area between July and November.

Several award-winning wineries depend on the well-drained soil and mild climate that nurtures their vineyards of French-American hybrids or vinifera grapes of Old World stock. After tours of wineries that were transformed from barns, tastings reveal fully aged and fruity flavors. Bottled wines are sold directly to the public.

Many farm markets raise annuals in greenhouses for residents to buy in the spring. This practice sparked a question that created a whole new industry with Pennslvania reigning as the number one producer in the nation: "What can we grow in the space under the seed flats?" In 1880, the answer from a Quaker farmer was, "Mushrooms!", now a $130 million Chester County industry that ships button mushrooms the length of the East Coast and as far west as the Mississippi.

Mushroom farming is precise. These edible fungi need a pasteurized environment to prevent the growth of *other* fungi. The process begins by mixing several agricultural by-products to make compost. Inside the mushroom house, this "soil" is purified with live steam. Then the beds are planted with pieces of mushroom spawn that were cultured in a lab as germ-free as an operating room. The farm staff tops the planted beds with sphaghnum moss, and growth proceeds in the building's darkness. From packing the beds to harvesting the snowy white buttons is an 11-week cycle.

About 100 farmers in Chester County raise mushrooms. The fourth generation of the Yeatman family is cultivating mushrooms on the same Avondale farm where they began in1921. It is labor-intensive agriculture that depends on meticulous care and climate-controlled houses but produces a harvest year-round.

"The green industry" or urban horticulture is major in the suburban sprawl around Philadelphia. The area features one of the largest concentration of botanicals outside of Great Britain. The sale of nursery stock alone—without the support industries such as landscape design—accounts for half of the $54 million that agriculture generates in Bucks County. Besides greenhouses selling direct to homeowners, several wholesalers raise shrubs and ornamental plants to ship to other states.

Farm families who say, "We've always been growers, and always will be," can sign onto the Pennsylvania Farmland Preservation Program and restrict their land to farm use permanently. In the mid-nineties about 100 farms totaling more than 8,800 acres in this region of the state were signed up for continuous agricultural use.

Full-time farming is being replaced by part-time or hobby farming, such as raising pheasants to release during hunting season or keeping horses for equestrian sports. Even though Chester County has lost almost half of the farms that it had 30 years ago, expansive fenced pastures with lanes leading to hilltop barns make it easy to believe that horses have a dominant role in this scenic county. Besides polo and fox hunts, steeplechase races and hunter trials proffer brilliant equestrian competition.

Horse-lovers compete in numerous events at the Devon Horse Show, which has been held on the Main Line, Route 30, each spring since 1896. A 100,000 spectators watch more than a thousand horses and ponies compete. Winners at the the country's oldest horse show could be our next Olympic medalists or World Cup champions.

The Radnor Hunt Fall Three-Day Event—a test of the combined skills of horse and rider in dressage, cross-country and stadium jumping—takes place when the fall foliage is at its peak.

Chester County Day invites 5,000 ticketholders to cruise scenic byways and tour restored homes filled with antiques and surrounded by artful gardens. Between stucco springhouses, stone meetinghouses and bank barns, lies a sense of heritage and respect for the land. One may see a gallery of original Penn land grants or a spreading oak close to three centuries old. These treasured endowments are unique to this area of Pennsylvania where Europeans first settled.

Honoring the land here implies faithfulness to its environmental and historic realities. It means managing land so that thickets protect creekbanks and wide views encompass field, farm and forest. Human involvement with the land here retains remnants of history within the present landscape. The old mills, forge ruins and covered bridges that dot the countryside west of Philadelphia teach residents about the area's past. The Brandywine Conservancy is a model for protecting water resources, saving and managing open space and preserving historic sites for future generations. Since its establishment in 1967, individuals have donated conservation easements and environmentally significant properties so that approximately 22,000 acres are protected in perpetuity. Future generations will enjoy the views within the Brandywine Valley that inspire people today as well as they did in the past.

What are the gifts of this countryside? The tall, old trees in the fencerow along Route 926. Jewelweed bobbing in the breeze near Doe Run. An orchard of frothy spring blossoms. Rhododendron blooming on the rocky cliff above River Road's sweep alongside the Delaware. A dip in a Chester County road with a barn with conical supports coming into view on the rise. Rolling meadows marked by tree-lined streams and white fences. Cows switching their tails as they chew their cud. Fog hugging a branch of the Brandywine and wrapping a covered bridge in its morning cloak. These are everyday views for the residents of Philadelphia's countryside; with Penn, they agree that "the country is to be preferred." They have taken the steps so that their offspring will enjoy the same inspiring environment.

*Following Pages* The rustic beauty of Cuttalossa Farm in upper Bucks County is sometimes used as a set.

*Top Left* Producing varietal wines from grapes grown in the rich soil of Brandywine country, Chaddsford Winery offers tours and tastings. *Center* Much of the beauty of the countryside around Philadelphia stems from Conservancy easements such as the Laurels Reserve where twin bridges cover Buck and Doe Runs. *Bottom* Visitors learn about a productive colonial farm at the Peter Wentz Farmstead in Montgomery County. *Above Right* Documented in tax records in the 1760s, the Moon-Williamson House in Fallsington, Bucks County, gives evidence of Quaker heritage and workmanship.

*Above* The flavor of Dilworthtown Country Store in Chester County reminds shoppers of bygone days. *Center* Mary Walls spins at the Colonial Pennsylvania Plantation, a self-sufficient 18th century farm located in Ridley Creek State Park. *Top Right* The Goschenhoppen Festival celebrates the living skills of the Schwenkfelders and other settlers who came to this Montgomery County valley in the 1700s. *Bottom* Wafers and fruit tarts look tempting at the Thomas Massey House, home of a Quaker settler of English descent, in Broomall, Delaware County.

*Previous Pages.* In areas farthest from Philadelphia farms like this one in Chester County continue to thrive. *Above Left* Masami Okamoto rides Fujiyama in the dressage competition of the annual Radnor Hunt Three-Day Event. *Center* Rolling hills and fenced meadows are hints of horse country. *Top Right* The Green Valley Farm near Doe Run is picturesque Chester County, the land of the fox hunt and the steeplechase. *Bottom* The Devon Horse Show, the oldest in the country, draws 100,000 spectators to its benefit event along the Main Line.

*TopLeft* Mills such as Keyser Mill at Evansburg
State Park in Montgomery County retain historic
value in the rural landscape beyond Philadelphia.
*Center* Ice and snow beautify the landscape.
*Bottom* Flowing from its source in Struble Lake,
Brandywine Creek West meanders through Hiber-
nia Park in Chester County. *Above* Sun sets on
a restored Bucks County farm. *Following Pages*
Rice's Market near Lahaska attracts buyers of produce,
flowers, crafts and anything else imaginable.

# THE LURE OF THE OUTDOORS

*On one of those Indian summer days that seem blessed by all the gods, it was fitting to head* towards John Heinz National Wildlife Refuge at Tinicum, a 900-acre spread in southwestern Philadelphia. Overhead, puffy clouds were sparse in the blue that spanned the downtown skyline, only six miles away. From the Visitor Contact Station, a trail atop a dike sliced the Darby Creek and a large, shallow pond. This freshwater stand and an adjacent tidal marsh lure birds travelling the Atlantic flyway. But, only a few ducks paddled in the slow-moving creek. On the other side, several waders meandered across the mud flats. The sun flitted with their reflections. Two egrets fished. Yellow seedheads bobbed above the water level, which is controlled by the refuge staff.

Near a spread of duckweed, a giant blue heron stood, listening attentively. The tension in his tail heightened. Was he going to fly? Instead, his beak plunged underwater and speared a feast-size fish. He struggled to retain his catch, balancing its wriggling weight against his body. Slowly he maneuvered through the shallows to terra firma to enjoy a gourmet alfresco in peace. Just another incident in the food chain of Philadelphia's wetlands.

The history of this preserve, renamed in 1991 to honor the late Senator Heinz, is literally earth moving. For ages, Darby Creek and the Schuylkill River have been depositing layers of sediment in the treeless lowlands bordering the Delaware. Its resulting fertility attracted the Swedes, the first European settlers here, in 1643. To drain lands for farming and cattle grazing, they built dikes throughout the area that is now the refuge. In the

*"Whatever men may say, our wilderness flourishes as a Garden, and our desert springs like a Greene field."*

*—William Penn*

20th century, hydraulic dredges sucked up this soil and filled in thousands of acres that now shoulder I-95, the shipyards, the international airport and housing developments.

When conservationists campaigned for some acreage to remain natural, the refuge was born. Reverse dredging recreated a filled marsh. Today, under the care of the U.S. Fish and Wildlife Service, the refuge attracts birders. They have sighted more than 280 species here. The birds enjoy duckweed and other aquatic plants in this natural oasis within an industrial landscape.

Birding is also a joy at Mill Grove, a lush, wooded setting in Montgomery County. This 175-acre farm/estate inspired the naturalist John James Audubon to be the first artist to portray birds and other wildlife in natural settings; he lived here for two years until 1806. Today, feeding stations, nesting boxes and plantings welcome more birds than the painter observed and collected. Miles of trails lead hikers along Perkiomen Creek and to the nearby Schuylkill River.

The Schuylkill, however, is better known for rowing, a sport marked by strenuous exercise and a tad of sophistication. Rugged individuals and collegiate teams row upriver and down in front of Boathouse Row, a line of worn clubhouses along Kelly Drive in Fairmount Park. Sleek fiberglass shells, at least 30 feet in length, cut gracefully through the water. There are several classes with some rowers sculling and others rowing sweep boats.

The most challenging class at the Schuylkill Regatta each fall is the "eights," the last race. Eight rowers depend on the cox for pace and rudder control as they pull the largest boat in competitive rowing through the wake. The team moves like one muscle. They even enter and exit the shell in unison. It isn't too surprising when the winner is Vesper, one of the more serious clubs on Boathouse Row. Here in Philadelphia the sport has a legacy. The Schuylkill Navy, an association of rowing clubs, was founded in 1858.

The bicycling community zooms in the Delaware Valley. Many cyclists enjoy the downhills of the open terrain at Valley Forge.

This national park, which was Pennsylvania's first state park, is linked to Philadelphia by the 22-mile Schuylkill Trail. Bicyclists thread along the river through urban blocks in Norristown and rural scenery in Plymouth Township on to the Manayunk Canal Tow Path and Fairmount Park. The bikeway is macadam and uncovers the Schuylkill River's past industrial connections.

There are other terrains for biking. Trails at Pennypack, a 1,300-acre park reaching from northeast Philadelphia into Montgomery County; the 10-foot-wide lane on the south side of the Ben Franklin Bridge across the Delaware and the 60-mile grassy path along the Delaware Canal are varied biking challenges. With their own risk and scenic factors, biking and trekking backroads will reveal the pulse of the local countryside.

Philadelphia's Fairmount Park has 20-some miles of bike trails, both gravel and paved. Some make up part of the 156-mile course of the Corestates-U.S. Pro Cycling Championship, a one-day race held in Philadelphia each June. Approximately 120 international pro cyclists compete. The grueling test of the loop is "the wall" on Lyceum Street in Manayunk that climbs almost a mile.

Horseback riding is a natural in several area state parks—Ridley Creek in Delaware County, French Creek in Chester and Tyler in Bucks. Riders can meander along wooded trails, slosh through creeks and gallop across grassy hills.

At the fields of the area's four polo clubs, the action is more vigorous for horse and player. No longer a sport limited to the male gentry, polo thrives with both sexes swinging their mallets. Polo came to the Philadelphia area in the forties and continues to grow locally as it does nationally. The short-field polo that is available through Doe Run and Bucks County Polo Clubs attracts players with only one horse. Brandywine, a well-established club started in 1949, plays arena and full-field polo. Spectators vote the Mallet Hill Club's field in Cochranville as the most scenic. The real players in this sport are the horses, but their riders get to unload the day's tension as they finish off the chuckers, or segments of the game. Both horses and humans are the winners.

Cricket, the precursor of baseball, arrived in the area in the mid-1800s. Its history includes strong association with Old Philadelphians, or the bluebloods who can trace their family to first settlers. The beautiful lawns at their clubs—Merion, Germantown and Philadelphia—have been usurped by lawn tennis.

The Delaware River, the cleanest major free-flowing river in the U.S., is a recreational draw. First-class fishing for stripers and bass is topped only by the shad that swim upriver in late March to spawn. Canoeing and kayaking interest some after the spring thaw; many more wait for hot weather.

Lazing with the current on an inflated raft or tube is a summer solace. The sky overhead, with an osprey silhouetted against it, arcs above the shoreline and the softly rippling water. From Upper Black Eddy in Bucks County, the float downstream to Point Pleasant is calm enough to mimic idleness. The river's width is 800 feet. Overnight camping on Treasure Island, one of the 11 islands in the vicinity, gives outdoor lovers a chance to see more of the wild. The Tohickon Creek has several rapids up to class four. It flows out of Nockamixon State Park, a botanical treasure of rocky cliffs, showy flowers and shaded ravines, and into the Delaware River.

The guided wildflower walks at Bowman's Hill Wildflower Preserve in Washington Crossing State Park display the wild wealth of Pennsylvania flora. On 80 acres, native plants flourish in their natural habitats. A favorite is the pond where aquatic creatures take shelter under spatterdock and arrowleaf. Along the edge, cardinal flower blooms under a swamp magnolia tree. Eight trails in this vicinity loop past wildflower stands that bloom anytime between March and October.

On a high slope, azaleas prosper. From this bluff during the Revolutionary War, Washington's General Lord Stirling decided that crossing the Delaware to surprise the enemy was a good gamble. Nowadays, a visit to Bowman's Hill always promises something alive and interesting to observe. From the indoor gallery, you can watch birds and butterflies feeding. At the right time of year, hummingbirds can be seen sipping nectar.

*Above* The grounds of Mill Grove, the home of artist/naturalist John James Audubon, offer excellent birding in Montgomery County. *Top Right* Sailing on the 535-acre lake at Marsh Creek State Park in Chester County is a summer pleasure. *Bottom* A giant blue heron spears a fish al fresco at the John Heinz National Wildlife Refuge at Tinicum, a mile or so from the site of the first European settlement in Pennsylvania.

*Above* The Delaware River offers a get-away for quiet canoeing as well as other water recreation. *Right* The paved trails at Valley Forge Historical National Park excite both the beginner and the experienced bicyclist. *Following Pages* In front of Boathouse Row in Philadelphia, the Schuylkill River is a highway for the sleek shells of scullers and rowers. As a sport, rowing here harks back to the 1800s.

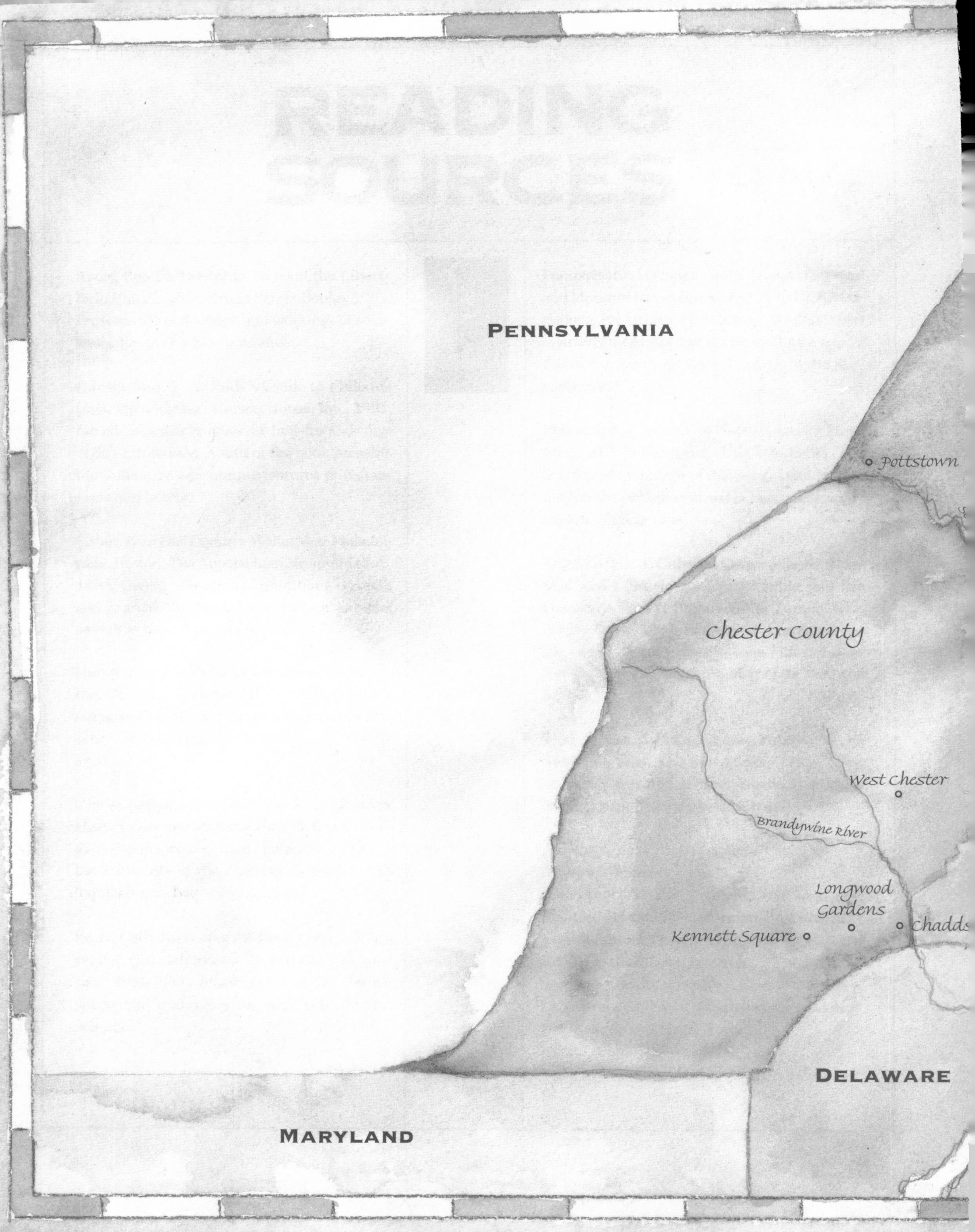

PENNSYLVANIA

Chester County

○ Pottstown

West Chester
○

Brandywine River

Longwood
Gardens
○

Kennett Square ○        ○ Chadds

DELAWARE

MARYLAND